T·O·W·N·A·N·D·C·I·T·Y·G·U·I·D·E·S
AA
GLASGOW
T·O·W·N·A·N·D·C·I·T·Y·G·U·I·D·E·S

The all-in-one guide to what goes on in and around the city

*Tourist information,
maps, walks, drives,
eating out, where to stay*

Produced by the Publishing Division of the Automobile Association

Cover: Drinks on the terrace in George Square with City Chambers in the background

Title page: Fish, ring, tree and bird on Glasgow's coat of arms are all associated with legends of Saint Mungo, the city's patron saint

Editor: Betty Sheldrick
Copy Editor: Joanna Jellinek
Art Editor: Bob Johnson
Design Assistant: K A G Design
Original Photography: Stephen Gibson, assisted by Pierre Guillemin
Picture Researcher: Wyn Voysey
Editorial Contributors: Patricia Bascom (Art Galleries and Museums); Ross Finlay (Glasgow's Green Places, City Centre: Places to Visit, Out of City: Places to Visit); Cliff Hanley (Introduction, The Story of Glasgow, Famous Glaswegians); Roger Smith (City Walks); Anthony Vogt (The City's Architecture); Roger Witts (The Performing Arts)

Directory compiled by Pam Stagg

Day Drives prepared by the Home Routes Research and Development Unit of the Automobile Association

Maps and plans produced by the Cartographic Department of the Automobile Association. Atlas based on the Ordnance Survey maps, reproduced with the permission of the controller of Her Majesty's Stationery Office. Crown copyright reserved.

Filmset by Vantage Photosetting Co Ltd, Eastleigh and London, England

Printed and bound by Graficromo SA, Spain

Produced and distributed in the United Kingdom by the Publishing Division of the Automobile Association, Fanum House, Basingstoke, Hampshire, RG21 2EA.

ISBN 0 86145 654 8
AA Reference 50733

CONTENTS

Introduction

In the ancient heart of Glasgow, Tron Steeple stands astride the pavement and the ages, linking a medieval past to the modern Tron Theatre that is in a converted church behind

Even Glaswegians will admit that every city is unique. And since Glasgow has always been very outward-looking, they recognise the peculiar charm of other places and applaud them.

An Edinburgh writer, reviewing a Glasgow book for the London *Times* newspaper, complained that the author had not noticed that Glasgow was an intensely American city. The author's response was that the fact was so clear it didn't seem worth mentioning. Situated on the west coast, and in its time a great seaport, Glasgow gave birth to both the stayers and the goers. There is scarcely a family in this city without cousins or second cousins in New York or Toronto, and those distant relations have a deep sentimental attachment to the place of their origins.

Like other great British industrial centres, it has had its wild ups and downs, and its character has learned to cope with them. Dear dirty Glasgow; the dear green place; the home of long-forgotten and hugely exaggerated little gang wars; the birthplace of the Industrial Revolution; the radical rebel town that created the legend of Red Clydeside. All the legends are true and not true. But what is true and enduring is the marvellous variety of the city.

As well as its Victorian slums, it created the imposing residences of the upper classes, it developed a passion for open spaces and parks, and it acquired an enthusiasm for the visual arts, for visionary architecture, for music and theatre.

What the visitor will certainly discover is the amiable and welcoming quality of the city. The friendliness of Glasgow is born of a tough self-confidence which feels no need to put other people down.

In recent years dear dirty Glasgow has got rid of its dirt, the legacy of that first Industrial Revolution, and has discovered the shining colours of fine old stone beneath. This has contributed to a delightful new pride in the city.

It will not surprise the reader that the contributors to this book seem quite besotted with their subjects. They have all drunk deep of Glasgow and are incurably intoxicated with the place. The book contains probably the best contemporary guide to those dear green places, Glasgow's parks, and a splendid selection of historical and pictorial walks for visitors who have caught the modern passion for the guarded use of their legs.

In area, as you will discover, Glasgow is quite a small, tidy city, so that its startling assembly of art galleries and museums are all within easy distance of the centre. And that assembly includes a constantly changing programme in the galleries of both universities, the superb collection at Kelvingrove, and the unique inheritance of the Burrell Collection. The book also introduces you to the astonishing assembly of the performing arts, while hinting slightly that the reason why they flourish may be that Glasgow itself is a piece of theatre.

Any strange city is a bafflement to a visiting driver, and Glasgow has its share of one-way streets and parking problems, but these are fewer than many cities', and a study of the maps should enable a visitor to avoid them. It is also a very easy place to get out of, and its hinterland has some of the most magical scenery in the world.

The book touches, not too solemnly, on the history that produced the Glasgow of today, since a city can't know what it is without knowing where it came from. Glasgow has certainly thrown up its fair quota of the great and the grotty; many of their contributions are still visible and tangible.

It is a city, like others, that has made massive mistakes. It has learned from them, and Glasgow encompasses a delightful marriage of the old and the recent and the new. In walking around town, don't keep your head down concentrating on this book, but look constantly up to first-floor level to see the dramatic decorations on the older buildings.

This book can, of course, be no more than a brisk introduction to a total experience. It will guide you to rich rewards. The wise traveller will keep eyes and ears open for the unexpected, and in Glasgow this is usually rewarding. The city is greater than the sum of its parts, and its people, as any open-minded traveller will certainly discover, are the greatest.

About this Book

Glasgow City Guide
Designed to be the complete guide for tourist or resident,
contains the following sections.

Features
Written by local experts, these introductory articles cover
subjects of special importance in the city — its history,
architecture, famous residents, its surprisingly numerous
parks, galleries and museums, and the arts scene.

City Centre: Places to Visit
Here places of interest, listed alphabetically, are described in
detail. Each entry includes its street name, so it can easily be
located on the street plan on page 104. For opening times
and practical information refer to the Directory.

City Walks
Six walks, with step-by-step route directions, have been
carefully planned to take in the best of the city. The chief
places of interest along the way are described in the text.

Out of City: Places to Visit
An alphabetical selection of the most attractive and
interesting towns, villages and places to visit in the
surrounding area. All within an hour or so's drive. For
opening times etc refer to the relevant section of the
Directory. Each entry has a grid reference, so can be located
on the maps on pages 98–101.

Day Drives
Two routes for exploring the countryside around the city,
including detailed route directions, a map and places of
interest.

District Maps
Four pages of mapping at a scale of 4 miles to the inch
covering the area around the city, extending approximately
30 miles from the city centre.

Throughroute Map
This shows the motorways and main roads in and out of the
city.

Glasgow City Plan
Large-scale map of the City Centre, with a street index and
places of interest clearly shown.

Directory
Eleven pages packed with useful information
grouped into sections (see page 118). All you need to know
about where to eat and stay, recreation, shops, sports and
services, plus useful addresses and opening times for all the
places of interest described in the book. A calendar of events
lists the major annual festivals, shows and sporting events
month by month.

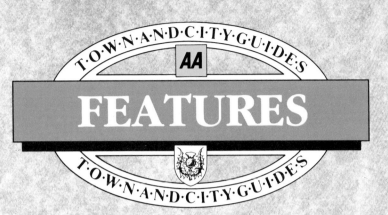

FEATURES

TOWN·AND·CITY·GUIDES

AA

TOWN·AND·CITY·GUIDES

*Shipyards on the Clyde, skeletal survivors from an era
when Glasgow harbour could claim to produce the biggest
and best ships in the world*

The Story
of
Glasgow

Traditionally the Second City of the Empire, Glasgow was also the 'dear dirty city', a mainspring of the first Industrial Revolution. No longer dirty, it is now (somewhat to its own surprise) a major tourist attraction.

THE ROMANS WERE HERE

To begin with there is a delightful variety of opinion about what Glasgow means. Depending on how the name was derived, it may mean Gray-hound, Gray-smith, Dark Glen, Black Church, Dear Green Place, Valley of Prayer, Sacred Glen. The natives survive this confusion with philosophical fortitude.

In Roman times an imperial road ran through Clydesdale, crossed the Molendinar Burn and ran along what is now Rottenrow. Two fords across the River Clyde led north to the High Street, and the Romans built a fort at the top of the street, where the Royal Infirmary now stands.

The conquest of Scotland was one of Rome's daftest whims. They lost an entire legion without trace, did not make a single denarius for the imperial coffers, and

probably caught a lot of colds. Parts of their Antonine Wall, built across the country, can still be detected in the area of Bearsden.

One local legend to explain the defeat of Rome is that the invaders stuck to their conventional tactic of marching in serried ranks with shields held vertically by the front phalanx and horizontally above the heads of succeeding ranks, forming what they called the *testudo*, or tortoise, which was designed to trample the enemy underfoot. This arrangement proceeded along the Gallowgate, where there was no enemy to trample, but from time to time an undersized native would nip out from a tenement close by, razor the legionary at the end of a rank and then vanish through the maze of back courts. This story needn't be taken too seriously—Glaswegians are good at spinning yarns!

What is true is that the Glaswegians of the time were Cymry, or Britons, part of the great westward drift of the Celtic people from Europe. They worshipped Baal, and some of the old rituals have drifted down to modern times in the customs of Hallowe'en and the reverence for mistletoe.

THE PREACHING OF THE WORD

With the end of the Roman experiment total darkness descends on the story of Scotland for several centuries. Nobody knows what this odd collection of tribes was up to during this time. History picks up the city again around AD400, when St Ninian, the Roman-educated Christian

missionary, is said to have set up the first cross of Glasgow. He didn't become Glasgow's patron saint. That was left to Mungo, or Kentigern, whose life has given the city some entertaining legends.

Early in the 5th century the Romans abandoned Britain entirely, and anarchy became the norm. A hundred years later, the story goes—and you may believe it or not, as you will—the great King Arthur drove savage Pictish invaders out to Strathclyde, and when the monarch was killed in battle at Camelon, near Falkirk, in 535, he was succeeded by his son Owen, or Eugene.

A fairly ubiquitous fellow, Arthur, you may complain. But Owen did exist; he married a lady called Thenew, whose people took a dislike to her and set her adrift in a coracle on the Firth of Forth to drift out to sea and drown. Divine intervention pushed the little boat upriver to Culross, where she gave birth to Mungo.

The boy was trained there by St Serf, became the teacher's pet, and so annoyed his fellow-pupils that they tried to kill his pet bird and they put out a fire he had been set to watch. The lad nursed the bird back to life and relit the fire by rubbing branches together. Both the bird and the burning bush figure in Glasgow's coat of arms.

There is also an even more dramatic story set in Glasgow itself. The King of Cadzow was sure his wife was having an affair; she did indeed give the knight in question a ring, a gift to her from the King. The King found the man asleep, took the ring from his satchel, hurled it into the Clyde, and told the Queen that he wanted her to wear it that same evening. She threw herself on Mungo's mercy. The good man sent a monk to fish in the river and bring back his first catch, which

turned out to be a salmon with the very ring in its mouth—naturally. The fish is also on the coat of arms; there may be a hint of scepticism in the jingle that goes with it:

Here's the tree that never grew, here's the bird that never flew, here's the bell that never rang, here's the fish that never swam.

Thenew is commemorated in the name St Enoch Square in the city centre. Mungo's tomb and well are to be found in the lower church of Glasgow Cathedral in the High Street. There were earlier cathedrals which were burned or razed. The present building dates back to only 1136, but as cathedrals go that is fairly venerable.

The burial ground adjacent, Glasgow Necropolis, is of much more recent date, faithfully modelled on the Père Lachaise Cemetery in Paris and commanded by a tall column topped by a statue of John Knox, the Protestant reformer, who appears to be shaking his fist at the church, which was of course originally Roman Catholic.

**GLASGOW
UNIVERSITY**
*Quadrangle typifying
George Gilbert Scott's
style, so much derided by the
'new wave' 1930s critics.
For students today a major
attraction of the old quad is
that from it one can see none
of the 20th-century
additions to Scott's design*

**MARY QUEEN OF
SCOTS**
*Bronze bust made when she
was about 18 years old,
shortly before her return to
Scotland on the death of her
French husband, Frances II*

HEROES AND MARTYRS

In another long period of nothing very much, we may note that Glasgow in 1175 became a burgh of barony under King William the Lion, which may have been fun at the time for the people who liked that sort of thing. Since the population was only about 3,000, it probably made good gossip. And there may well have been wild excitement when in 1242 the place obtained from Alexander II the right of free trade through Lennox and Argyll. These things obviously mattered at the time, whatever we may think of them now.

Rather more important was Glasgow's connection with William Wallace, the patriot from Paisley who did his best to wrest freedom from the English yoke, and wasn't too well supported by the Scottish aristocracy because he was a mere knight and not a big landowner. It was Wallace who captured the the Bishop's Palace from the English, and it was in a Glasgow suburb, Robroyston, that he was defeated by the Southerners and whisked to London, to be accused of treason and brutally done to death.

Mary Queen of Scots took her leave of Scotland in the city. The year was 1568. Forced to abdicate the throne in favour of her extremely unremarkable son, James VI, she headed for Dumbarton Castle. The Earl of Moray rushed to intercept her people, and they clashed at Langside. Mary watched the fray from Cathcart Castle. The Queen's men lost. She was able to flee to London and the protection of her cousin, Elizabeth, who had her locked up for 19 years and then beheaded.

Mary had written the infamous Casket Letter to the Earl of Bothwell, which proved her treachery to the English Queen—or was it a forgery? She wrote it—or did she?—in Provand's Lordship, the oldest dwelling house in Glasgow. Mary may have stayed there while she was taking her pathetic husband, Darnley, back to Edinburgh, a journey which he interrupted to stay overnight in Kirk o' Field, where he was murdered and the house blown up, almost certainly by the Earl of Bothwell.

Bonnie Prince Charlie, Charles Edward Stuart, was a perfect nuisance to Glasgow. In his campaign to recapture the British throne in 1745, he conquered Edinburgh and wrote to Glasgow demanding campaign money. The Council coughed up £5,000.

When the Prince abandoned his invasion of England, he came back to Glasgow and asked for more. He got £10,000 and thousands of shirts and waistcoats, stockings and trousers, and held a brave review on Glasgow Green. He lived in Glasgow's most splendid house, Shawfield Mansion at the corner of Glassford Street and Trongate, and dined twice daily in public to let his future subjects admire. On 3 January 1746 he took his army away, to crushing defeat and his exile.

THE LUST FOR LEARNING

The High Street was certainly the centre of things in Glasgow. The Tolbooth Steeple, at its foot, still stands to recall the Tolbooth's functions as courthouse and jail. Outside this building public executions were a popular entertainment; for lesser crimes this was the starting point from which miscreants were dragged through the city behind a cart, with occasional resting spots where they would be flogged.

A little to the north the city established its first university in 1451; the third in Scotland after St Andrews and Aberdeen. The site is now a railway yard. In 1870 the institution moved to Gilmorehill in the West End, to a building designed by Sir George Gilbert Scott. It was considered splendid at the time. In the 1930s architectural critics, falling under the influence of Le Corbusier and the Bauhaus school, dismissed it as wedding-cake architecture. (It was Le Corbusier who called a house 'a machine for living in', on the odd assumption that human beings are cogs and pistons.) The 20th-century additions to the Yoonie, as Glaswegians call it, are wonderful Bauhaus conceptions, marvellously ugly, high-rise and unfunctional. The Gilbert Scott original is a delight to be seen.

The university helped to mother the first Industrial Revolution. Joseph Black's thesis on latent heat, which probably qualifies him as the father of chemistry, led a humble artisan in the university, James Watt, to make the steam-engine a working proposition. The work of William Thompson, later Lord Kelvin, made possible the transatlantic cable and many other wonders.

THE CLYDE MADE GLASGOW

. . . and Glasgow made the Clyde. It made both the river and itself black with soot and grime, as the city raced into a commanding position in the first Industrial Revolution. Its shipyards were supreme, and 'Clyde-built' was a global guarantee of quality. Was the *Queen Mary* the greatest ship ever built? Maybe. She was only one of thousands launched, rather improbably, into the narrow, shallow stream, usually with hundreds of tons of massive chain trailing behind them to prevent them from sailing up the opposite bank.

NEW LOOK GLASGOW

To ensure the health of future generations of Glaswegians, the country parks of the region offer sailboarding and other fun and fitness leisure pursuits

THE BROOMIELAW

Below: passengers embark on paddle steamers at the Broomielaw. This was the dock for trips 'doon the watter' to the Firth of Clyde. Some Victorian businessmen commuted daily from resorts such as Dunoon and Rothesay

Glasgow was a producer of big heavy industrial material, and its population leapt from under 80,000 in 1801 to over 700,000 in 1901. It was to top a million in the present century before easing back to 800,000. The increase wasn't simply a question of birth rate—that was high, but infant mortality was horrifying. There were huge intakes from the impoverished Highlands and Islands, and massive immigrations from Ireland during the potato famine of the 1840s and again at the turn of the century. The city swelled, with a proliferation of congested slums and poverty alongside the exuberant industry and its making of millionaires. But in spite of the hardship, or maybe because of it, the city held on to its resilience and its black humour—black to match the grime-covered tenements. In recent memory the view of Glasgow from the hills to north or south was simply an enormous mound of smoke. Tuberculosis was the resident killer.

None of this prevented Glasgow from throwing up magnificent galleries and concert halls, launching the Great Exhibitions of 1911 and 1938 and, on another level, going crazy about dancing. In the great days of ballroom dancing, Glasgow was the world leader; alongside the sprawl of elegant *palais de danse*, every hall in the place became a dance hall at weekends.

The dance craze ran its course and vanished. So did the heavy industries. So did the grime, after the postwar passing of the Clean Air Act.

THE NEW LOOK

Glasgow always had the advantage over London and some other cities of being easy to get out of, and its easily accessible hinterland was virtually untouched by the industrial pall. The rolling hills of Strathclyde all round were, as they still are, a delight to the eye, and the industrial muck of the Clyde dissipated easily in the tidal waters of the Firth. Flanked by stern hills and sprinkled with islands, the Firth of Clyde became the city's lungs every summer, with couthy resorts such as Largs and Dunoon and Rothesay and Millport and Tighnabruaich.

Cheap package holidays in Europe have changed that, but the Firth still has its magnetism for visitors from outside Scotland. It is also one of the finest yachting waters in the world.

BARKING AT THE BROOMIELAW, GLASGOW. 5066. G.W.W.

The city's own old grimy face has been transformed. The postwar urge to solve the age-old housing shortage produced, as elsewhere, the gruesome spectacle of virtually uninhabitable skyscrapers to be hurried past with averted eyes. But in the subsequent reaction, and with clean air, Glaswegians were seized with a mania for rehabilitating the old tenements and sandblasting them to reveal the original honey-gold or pink sandstone, which is almost luminous. They were reclaiming their heartland.

Poet Laureate John Betjeman, an architectural enthusiast, described Glasgow as the greatest Victorian city in Europe, at at time when Victorianism had a bad name. He would admire it even more now that it shines in the light.

In place of the sooty clamour of industry, the Clyde has adopted a welcoming face, with its new walkway, a great exhibition centre and a site for the 1988 Garden Festival. It has also cleaned up its own act, and salmon have been sighted in the heart of the city where once all fishy creatures had disappeared.

THINGS OF THE SPIRIT

Glasgow is the home of the Scottish National Orchestra as well as of the BBC Scottish Symphony Orchestra, the Scottish Opera and the Scottish Ballet, these last three based at the magnificent Theatre Royal. The splendid old King's Theatre survives to house touring companies and exuberant local amateurs, and even a form of music-hall survives at the Pavilion.

It has its resident rep company at the Citizens' and proliferates small companies in houses like the Tron and the Mitchell and the Third Eye Centre.

The Kelvingrove galleries house the finest art collection in Britain outside London, and the new Burrell Collection, in lush parkland to the south of the river, is one of Britain's top tourist attractions. Largely overlooked by visitors, though loved by the natives, is the People's Palace on Glasgow Green, which ignores the 'higher' things of life and preserves the short and simple annals of the poor.

But even outside of these, the city itself is a kind of living theatre. Probably because it has known so many hard times, it is one of the friendliest places in the world, as even the people of Edinburgh declare. Its easy humour will survive current industrial problems. How it changes next is another history.

Cliff Hanley is a Glasgow journalist and broadcaster, and has written several books on Glasgow and Scotland.

Couthy: *friendly; comfortable*

KING'S THEATRE
Opened in 1904, the King's Theatre was a fit ambience for Glasgow's respectable Edwardian bourgeoisie. It survives and thrives, now owned by the local authority

---

PEOPLE'S PALACE
Stained glass—a part of Glasgow's social history— in the People's Palace

The City's Architecture

Glasgow is unique among British cities, having been a world centre for that short but imaginative period of architecture known as the Art Nouveau. Much of this fame stems from the work of Charles Rennie Mackintosh, but Glasgow is rich too in older architecture, for it has been prosperous since the Middle Ages.

IRONWORK
The city's coat of arms, portrayed with elegance and charm near Glasgow Cathedral. The bell represents one St Mungo brought from Rome

NECROPOLIS
John Knox, mounted on a Doric column, and fellow monuments

MERCHANTS' HOUSE
In George Square: the Ship of Trade (a replica of one in Briggait, where the Merchants' House once stood) celebrates trading success

Glasgow has consistently swept away the old and built new. This process gives a compact diverse city with only the very good or fortunate buildings surviving.

ORIGINS
As with many old cities the Church and the University were the seeds of growth. Glasgow Cathedral was founded by St Mungo in the 6th century but the building we see today dates from the 12th century, and was heavily restored in the 19th century. Owing to its steeply sloping site, the building is 'split-level' with a raised choir and a massive stone undercroft that supports this east end. The adjacent Necropolis provides a fascinating and macabre insight into the Victorian attitude to the dead, as well as fine views over the city.

In front of the cathedral the Bishop's Palace is now undergoing archaeological work. Adjacent is the last remaining medieval house, Provand's Lordship, now a museum showing Glasgow life of the period. The name High Street survives, but only imagination and old pictures can restore the vision of the medieval street running down the hill packed with similar houses, past the original university and the tall elegant 17th-century Tolbooth Steeple to the river.

A small, but elegant, Georgian development grafted itself on to the lower end of this spine. The best remaining buildings are St Andrew's Church, with a fine tall spire, and, just across the River Clyde, Carlton Place, a quite regular façade of typical Georgian proportions, making good use of its river frontage.

THE GREAT EXPANSION
Glasgow's 'big bang' started about 1800, and the city continued to grow at an ever-increasing rate for nearly 100 years. The thousands of closely packed, solid stone buildings—with walls seldom less than 2ft (600mm) thick, every stone hand-cut to fit on to the next and usually completed with fine carving—represent the supreme human effort involved during this period of rapid expansion.

The town developed on a gridiron plan, broken only for very special buildings or by the occasional, already existing road. This rigid framework, relieved by the hilly terrain, contrasts with the buildings, which are of every imaginable style, size and type. This gridiron street pattern, coupled with the Scottish use of urban dwellings divided into flats, made Glasgow very different from other British cities.

Any city built mainly in the 19th century is bound to glory in the Victorian love of mixing historic styles of architecture, and Glasgow does this with great gusto. The change from Georgian order to Victorian energy occurs in the Merchant City area where two buildings are allowed to interrupt the grid. Stirling's Library (formerly the Royal Exchange) sits in the controlled, regular Royal Exchange Square, with symmetrical arches leading to Buchanan Street. St George's Tron Church in Nelson Mandela Place (formerly St George's Place), on the other hand, is surrounded by five different buildings, each in its own style and colour ranging from off-white to deep red stone. The south side of the square is dominated by John Burnet's Venetian Gothic Stock Exchange; facing it on the north side is his son's (Sir John James Burnet) classical Atheneum, in a gentlemanly grey stone topped by very fine sculptures.

Around this group of buildings is the architectural heart of the city with towering, ornate walls of intricately carved stone, imposing entrance portals and decorative ironwork. Few now have their interiors intact, but the red Dumfriesshire sandstone and brick building on the corner of West Regent Street and Renfield Street houses an elegant restaurant known as De Quincey's, where, during alterations a few years ago, the original tiled interior was discovered virtually intact under layers of more modern work! Fortunately the owner decided to restore the subtle green, white and buff embossed tiles that cover every surface and recreate the atmosphere associated with the traditional palm court.

Westwards at the top of a rise, the totally regular Blythswood Square commemorates the original landowners. Just past the square stands St Vincent Street Church by Alexander 'Greek' Thomson, 'Greek' because of his love of the ornamentation and composition styles of that country. He was a technical innovator, using plate glass to achieve clear openings in his buildings and he used the classic vocabulary in new ways. St Vincent Street Church is due for renovation; however, under the grime it is still possible to appreciate the composition of the building. On a great block of a podium stands the solid classical church with its massive but very personal tower, producing a fine silhouette from many parts of the city.

CITY INSTITUTIONS

As Glasgow grew, so its institutions were built to reflect their prestige. The City Chambers in George Square, opened in 1888 by Queen Victoria, are ornate from the outside and have a lavish interior. The central hall and double staircase with marble pillars, painted ceilings and mosaic floors provide an awe-inspiring foretaste of the many grandiose rooms—and the decor even extends to the original loos!

CITY CHAMBERS
The central hall, with starkly imposing marble and alabaster staircase, granite columns and vaulted, elaborately decorated ceiling, recalls a Renaissance interior. The Victorian relish for opulence is somewhat tempered here by a taste for refinement; but this building, designed as a magnificent centrepiece for the city, boldly epitomises a period when Victorian confidence was at its height in the 'second city of the Empire'

The Clyde Port Authority is splendidly housed beside the river. Built by Sir John James Burnet, using maritime motifs such as ship prows instead of the usual derived decoration of the period, it is topped by exceptional sculptures, including Britannia and Neptune.

Glasgow University, founded in 1451, made an unusual decision after 400 years of its existence to sell up its historic lands on the cramped High Street and build grand new premises in the open fields of Gilmorehill. No other of our ancient universities has made such a bold move, but then none has found itself in such a thriving and rapidly expanding city. Only a few pieces of its ancient hallowed buildings were moved to the new site. However, it now has a major group of 19th-century buildings by Sir George Gilbert Scott in a Gothic Revival style, freely mixing traditional stone, cast-iron and plate glass to create new and daring effects.

A NUMBER OF CURIOS

It is impossible to leave the 19th century without mentioning a couple of the odd buildings that Glasgow has collected. A certain Mr Kibble had a fine domed glasshouse, 146ft (45m) in diameter, in his back garden, which was so admired for its elegant form and unbelievably delicate structure that he eventually gave it to the city in 1870 on condition that it was placed in the fashionable West End and that he could have the use of it as a winter garden for 20 years. Later additions have been made to the re-erected glasshouse, but otherwise the structure has stood the test of time well. Some of the original glass remains, giving delicate pink and green hues unlike the 'perfect' glass of today.

Templeton, a carpet manufacturer, had a fine building site alongside the historic Glasgow Green. The city fathers refused to have a factory in such a prominent position. In desperation, Templeton commissioned the architect, William Leiper, saying simply 'get us permission'. Leiper responded by modelling the factory on the Doges' Palace in Venice, using multicoloured glazed bricks and tiling instead of the delicate pink and white marble of the original. The result stands today as a 'rip-off' that perhaps more factories could emulate! A clever extension carried out in the 1920s to the right of the main façade is in the Art Deco style but complements Leiper's work perfectly.

THE CLIMAX OF THE EDWARDIAN AGE

Late 19-century Glasgow had risen to be the second city of the British Empire with a population of over one million. The confidence this generated was shown by the vision of its architects; the city's Art Nouveau buildings, in particular, rank as world class. Although Charles Rennie Mackintosh is undoubtedly the foremost architect of that time, he was not alone; James Salmon's eccentrically carved 'Hatrack' building at 142 St Vincent Street, and the early (1905) reinforced concrete building, Lion Chambers, in Hope Street are certainly very special office blocks.

Mackintosh was not a prolific builder but undoubtedly a unique creative genius. Examples of his work in the city are easily accessible and display his range of talents well. Queen's Cross Church, at 866 Garscube Road, was built in 1897, and is now the home of the Charles Rennie Mackintosh Society. The Willow Tearooms, 217 Sauchiehall Street, were one of several such establishments designed by Mackintosh for the formidable Kate Cranston, whose name is synonymous with the introduction of tea rooms to Glasgow. The interior has been recently restored, and the first-floor tea room is virtually original.

The Hunterian Art Gallery of Glasgow University has recently recreated Mackintosh's home. Here one can see the charming but cavalier manner in which he and his artist wife, Margaret Macdonald, restyled the old home with many elegant pieces of his furniture, together with books, pictures and some of his famed flower arrangements. Seen against the average Edwardian interior, it was shocking and exciting—today it looks simply very, very elegant.

Mackintosh's masterpiece is the Glasgow School of Art. The result of a competition, it was built in two stages, starting in 1897. The straightforward plan is carried through with creative passion; every piece of stone or wood is carved, metal forged, and light manipulated to enhance the spaces. All the halls and corridors are lined in dark timber so that doors leading to major rooms open into a

•─●●─•

CHARLES RENNIE MACKINTOSH
Mackintosh poster and replicas of stencilled banners in the Hunterian Art Gallery. The photograph (above) shows Mackintosh aged about 35

•─●●─•

burst of light reflected from the white walls. This effect is heightened by the often amusing coloured glass 'eyes' let into the doors and back lit from the rooms.

The second stage, finished in 1907, fits perfectly with the first, but on examining it one finds that the extra time has allowed Mackintosh's imagination to run further. This work owes nothing to tradition; all is fresh and unique. The west end tower represents the culmination, with the library its jewel. A double-height room, its bookstack (an afterthought by the client) is suspended in the upper volume, leaving just enough height for a gallery in the main library. The bookstack now houses the school's Mackintosh furniture exhibition. The main library manages to combine drama in its architecture with calm in its atmosphere.

INTO THE 20TH CENTURY

With a decline in industry and a falling population, the city's building industry has not flourished this century. The only area to boom was the cinema; Glasgow had over 130 by the late 1930s. Many were excellent examples of popularist Art Deco, but unfortunately, many have disappeared with the decline in cinema audiences.

Over the past few years, a reviving prosperity has brought much environmental improvement, the Woodlands district being a good example, and new buildings of merit. The Burrell Collection building in Pollok Park, finished in 1983, is the outstanding example. The winner of the specially organised architectural competition, Barry Gasson's design brilliantly solved the awkward requirement of housing three complete rooms from Sir William Burrell's home, Hutton Castle, by placing them around an internal courtyard. The entire length of the long gallery next to the adjacent woods is glazed, so that every day the sun's passage changes the decor and every season the trees redecorate this wall.

Medieval stone portals, a Tudor oak ceiling and stained-glass windows have been incorporated into the timber, stone and glass building, where they are displayed to their maximum advantage.

The future holds prospects of general improvement and certainly two major new buildings. The Royal College of Music and Drama will shortly move from their outdated Burnet buildings to new ones in Renfrew Street by Sir Leslie Martin, and the city is committed to a new major concert hall by 1990.

Anthony Vogt is Director of Graduate Studies at the Mackintosh School of Architecture.

Art Nouveau: *a style of architecture prevalent around the turn of the century. Sinuous curves are combined with strict geometry.*

undercroft: *a heavily vaulted lower room under the normal floor of a church*

Gridiron plan: *streets cross at right angles giving rise to equal 'sizes' of all plots*

John James Burnet (son): *the first Glasgow architect to attend the world-famous Beaux Arts school in Paris. His practice ended as one of the largest in Britain with offices in London, Glasgow, USA and South Africa.*

Dumfriesshire sandstone: *This deep red stone replaced the pale buff-grey local sandstone, which was exhausted by the end of the 19th century. This colour change is an easy guide to the date of buildings of the period.*

Art Deco: *a style of early modernism with ornament based on popular motifs from jazz, Egyptian and Red Indian sources*

Glasgow's Green Places

First-time visitors to Glasgow sometimes arrive under the misapprehension that they are about to see nothing but close-packed buildings. In fact, Glasgow has a greater number of parks per head of population than any other city in Europe. The derivation of its original Celtic name—'the dear green place'—is not just a creation of the city's famously hyperactive public relations department.

Victorian Glaswegians, in particular, really loved their parks. A census in 1893, when the city had only nine public parks, showed that 204,693 people had visited them—on 6 August alone.

Although the rate of visitors per day is no longer at that astonishing level, Glasgow District—which is slightly larger than the old City of Glasgow as it existed when local government boundaries were redrawn in 1975—now includes more than 70 public parks. There are eight public golf courses within its borders, and almost as many private ones; dozens of public and private bowling greens; sports grounds for football, rugby, athletics, cricket and shinty, the fast tough Highland game resembling hockey.

GLASGOW GREEN—FIRST PARK FOR THE PEOPLE

Back in medieval times, Glasgow was centred on the cathedral, which had long since taken the place of St Kentigern's tiny 6th-century church beside the tumbling Molendinar Burn. The private gardens and orchards of the clergy rose from the banks of the burn.

Lower down its course, where the Molendinar flattened out before flowing into the River Clyde, the level grasslands of Glasgow Green were common land, mentioned as early as 1178 as being where the humbler citizens grazed their cattle and sheep. In 1662 Glasgow Corporation offically adopted the Green as the city's first public park.

The ordinary folk of Glasgow dried their washing and bleached their linen on the Green. Bonnie Prince Charlie's Jacobite army camped on it. James Watt was strolling across the Green when he had the flash of inspiration which led to his redesign of the steam-engine and ushered in the Industrial Revolution.

Victorian Glasgow came here to disport itself among the discreet bathing boxes on the banks of the Clyde. Circuses, carnivals and ramshackle wooden theatres were all located here. Great political demonstrations and fiery orators haranguing the crowds at Glasgow's equivalent of Hyde Park are all part of the Green's history. And yet 19th-century speculators—even the Corporation itself—promoted baleful schemes to build a railway across the Green, to mine it for coal and then have the excavations used as a rubbish tip.

But the real story of Glasgow Green is not concerned with unscrupulous

businessmen, politicians, armies or great historical figures. It is the story of ordinary folk, and no more appropriate place than this could have been chosen for the People's Palace, opened in 1898 and, of all Glasgow's museums, the one most closely linked with the social history of the city itself.

VICTORIAN ENTHUSIASM FOR PARKS

Despite its long involvement with Glasgow Green, it was only in 1852 that the Corporation took over its second park, buying 85 acres of land on the banks of the River Kelvin, on what was then the city's western edge.

In 1888 and again in 1901, literally millions of visitors wandered round the Great International Exhibitions in Kelvingrove Park. Gondolas cruised on the river, and cable cars ran from the riverside to the high ground of the elegant Park Terrace on the north-east skyline. These exhibitions were a very shrewd investment by the city fathers. The profits paid for the sandstone extravaganza of Kelvingrove Art Gallery and Museum, which opened in 1903.

In the 1850s, as work on Kelvingrove Park began, Glasgow started on a parkland acquisition spree. Several of the properties deliberately occupy commanding hilltop sites. Notable among these is Queen's Park, in a district where local names like Battlefield recall a violent past. The park is named after Mary Queen of Scots. It occupies the site where, on 13 May 1568, her army was defeated at the Battle of Langside and she began her long slow journey to abdication, exile and execution.

At the time when it was added to the city's 'portfolio', Queen's Park was well out in the country. Even farther away was the ridgetop Cathkin Braes Park, gifted in 1886. At almost 600ft (183m) above sea level it has a magnificent view over the whole of the city, the Kilsyth, Campsie and Kilpatrick Hills to the north, and away beyond them to the mountains of the Highland Line. James White, the belting

HOGGANFIELD LOCH
The loch includes an island bird sanctuary

VICTORIA PARK
The Fossil Grove is a prime attraction in Victoria Park, and the disused quarry in which the fossilised tree stumps were discovered by accident in 1880 is now a rock- and water-garden

LINN PARK
It would be hard to cross this bridge over the White Cart Water in Linn Park without pausing for reflection. The park has woods and open land along the banks of the winding river. It was from Court Hill on the northern side of the park that Mary Queen of Scots watched the fateful Battle of Langside

and boots manufacturer who gave the Braes to the city, made it a condition that no gardens or sports grounds should be provided. He wanted the park to remain in its original moor and woodland state; and so it has, right to the present day.

Just after Cathkin Braes came to the city, the separate burgh of Partick—west of Kelvingrove but soon to be absorbed in the expanding city of Glasgow—laid out Victoria Park. This became very popular thanks to its formal and rock gardens, and its model-yacht and boating pond with islands and footbridges. But the most remarkable feature of Victoria Park is the Fossil Grove. Excavations to build a footpath at the south-west corner of the park uncovered a layer of 330-million-year-old fossilised tree stumps, now housed and protected in their own special display building.

The enthusiasm of the Parks Department for high-level viewpoints reappeared in the 1890s. Bellahouston Park was centred on a long wooded ridge, while Ruchill Park was the scene of a spirited response to outside pressure.

Ruchill Park's highest point should have offered an all-round panoramic view. But the owner of the ground to the south-east built a tenement block which obscured the whole outlook in that direction. James Whitton, who had just come from being head gardener at Glamis Castle to take charge of the city's parks, was having none of it. He used 24,000 cartloads of rubble from nearby building sites to create an artificial hilltop well above the roof level of the offending tenements, and then ran a spiral footpath to the summit. In celebration of his achievement, the artificial hill was nicknamed Ben Whitton; and the row of tenements which caused all the trouble are in what is now called Benview Street.

BETWEEN THE WARS

After the First World War, Linn Estate on the south side of the city was taken over to provide a wooded park on both banks of the White Cart Water. Long before the suburbs encroached on it, this riverside had been a popular recreational area. One of the Glasgow School of artists, Sir John Lavery, had a great success in 1886 with an evocative painting of a lazy-day tennis party at Cartbank, a work which is, curiously enough, not in the city's own spectacular art collection but in Aberdeen Art Gallery.

While Linn Park was being laid out, Hogganfield Park was being created on the city's north-eastern edge. This was an intriguing link with the very first public park of them all. Hogganfield Loch is the source of the Molendinar Burn, which, although it is nowadays mostly culverted and out of sight, still wanders into the city centre, passes the cathedral and flows into the Clyde at Glasgow Green.

Other between-the-wars acquisitions included Knightswood Park, which now has the city's busiest publicly owned golf course, and King's Park, accepted as a gift in 1930. But the most remarkable offering in the parkland line was to come after the Second World War.

THE POLLOK ESTATE

Pollok Estate had been the home for 700 years of the Maxwell family, latterly the Maxwell Macdonalds. They had made several gifts of parkland ground to the city, and since 1911 most of their beautifully wooded private estate had been open to the public.

All of this was surpassed in 1966, when the Maxwell Macdonalds made over the remaining 361 acres of Pollok Estate to the city, including the stately Palladian mansion of Pollok House.

The estate is now a country park. Pollok House, with its fine furnishings and paintings, is a museum. And the Burrell Collection, opened in 1983, housing Sir William Burrell's remarkable art treasures, attracts worldwide attention. No wonder that more than a million visitors come to Pollok every year.

SMALL-SCALE ATTRACTIONS

But Glasgow thinks in smaller terms as well. In 1970 a much-loved West End feature seemed to be threatened by the building of a hotel. Bingham's Pond, alongside Great Western Road, had once been the winter base of the Glasgow Western Skating Club and was used for boating in summer. Although reduced in size and 'municipalised' away from its older-fashioned rustic appearance, Bingham's Pond Park at least survives.

Some of Glasgow's green places are neither developed nor even particularly attractive.

But locations like Possil Loch, the majestically named Auchenshuggle Wood and the derelict Cunningar Loop on the Clyde at Dalmarnock have their own interest and their own enthusiasts as nature reserves.

There are famous individual trees, too, like the Darnley Sycamore in a railed-off enclosure beside Nitshill Road. On that spot tradition claims Mary Queen of Scots nursed her husband, Lord Darnley, during his serious illness in the summer of 1565. If ever a tradition seemed suspect, this is it. Darnley's family seat was at Crookston Castle, only a mile and a half away, so it is highly unlikely that he would be convalescing anywhere else. And recent trial borings make it clear that the tree itself was planted around the year 1800. But the commitment to preserve the sycamore is there, and it is accepted.

In the 1850s, one of the families who lived in the newly built tenement house at 1223 Argyle Street planted a clump of primroses in their front garden. Unknown to them, the earth around the primrose roots contained a little ash-tree seed. After 130-odd years, the tiny garden—no more than four paces wide—harbours an ash tree whose crown soars high above the roof of the four-storey building beside it. In many ways the tree must be an inconvenience. But it will never be cut down.

At an entirely different elevation, Glasgow has a fixation about crocuses. Every springtime millions of them, it seems, enliven not only the parks but also odd corners of city streets and grassy roadside bankings.

THE NATIONAL GARDEN FESTIVAL

If these are modest examples of 'green places' in the city, the Parks and Recreation Department is never happier than when flexing its muscles on some much more substantial project. As soon as it was announced that Glasgow was to be the location of the National Garden Festival in 1988, civic authorities and private companies alike began to pour money, expertise and a lot of hard work into the operation.

The derelict Prince's Dock site on the south bank of the Clyde was earmarked for the Festival. On its 120 acres something like 85,000 trees and 350,000 flowering shrubs were planted—and these numbers do not include the ones laid down by individual exhibitors.

A wildlife garden, a 240ft (73m) viewing tower with revolving glass elevator, train and tramway systems, a £1.2 million pedestrian bridge across the Clyde from the Scottish Exhibition and Conference Centre on the north bank—it quickly became a project on the scale of the International Exhibitions in Kelvingrove and the still-remembered Empire Exhibition at Bellahouston Park in 1938.

By 1989 the Garden Festival will be only a memory. The Prince's Dock site will be rebuilt yet again for housing. And Glasgow will have its eye set on some other project to make sure that its ancient status as 'the dear green place' still shows no sign of going by default.

Ross Finlay is a freelance writer and broadcaster.

HOGGANFIELD PARK

Rowing boats are for hire, the park contains an excellent 18-hole golf course and bird watching and coarse fishing are other activities to be indulged in. Ever since it was opened in 1920, this park in the north-easterly suburbs of Glasgow has been a popular place for family outings

Art Galleries
&
Museums

'Something for everyone' is a sweeping claim that is amply justified by the rich variety and wide scope of the museums and galleries in the city.

THE McLELLAN BEQUEST

In Glasgow, contrary to popular belief, there is a long tradition of interest in the visual arts. The splendid medieval cathedral, the elaborate monuments of the neighbouring Necropolis, the rich and confident architecture of the merchant city and the later public buildings, the Victorian and Edwardian mansions of the West End and South Side speak in their different ways of people who liked what was good and chose it for themselves and for their city.

No less do the contents of those houses reflect an interest in art and a determination to possess and to cultivate it. So it is that the city owes the nucleus of its famous collection of paintings to Archibald McLellan, a coach-builder and Deacon Convenor of the Trades House. During a busy life he amassed a notable collection of paintings and had a gallery built in which they could be viewed by his fellow citizens. On his death he bequeathed both the paintings and the building (which still stands on Sauchiehall Street) to the city. Unfortunately he died insolvent and the city fathers had to agree to pay his creditors. Thus, in 1854 the people of Glasgow acquired the paintings for £15,000 (including *The adulteress brought before Christ* by Giorgione) and the McLellan gallery building for £29,500.

For some time the paintings remained on view there. Then, as the city's other collections grew, a small mansion house, built to a design by Robert Adam near the River Kelvin about three miles west of the city centre, was purchased for the display of historic and scientific items of interest. The people of Glasgow were able to continue to cultivate the admirable habit of museum visiting.

THE MUSEUM PROJECT

The West End of the city became its academic centre soon afterwards with the removal of Glasgow University from High Street to Gilmorehill. From there the university's impressive towered and turreted structure by Sir George Gilbert Scott looked down to Kelvingrove House among the trees. After the addition of a new wing to the house in 1876, to display technological material, it was decided that a new building was required in which all the collections could be on view together.

This project was conceived on a grand scale and a Great International Exhibition was planned for 1888 to raise the necessary funds. The venue of the exhibition was Kelvingrove Park and it embraced industrial and artistic concepts, with

sections entitled The Queen's Presents, The Picture Gallery, The Bishop's Castle, Women's Industries and many others. It was very popular and the sum of £46,000 was made available for the new museum.

Next came a competition for the design of the building. This was launched in 1891 under the auspices of a society calling itself the Association for the Promotion of Arts and Music. According to the original brief, the building was also to include a concert hall and a school of art. This latter idea was dropped and a separate competition was launched in 1895 for a design for the Glasgow School of Art. This was won by a firm of Glasgow architects, with designs by Charles Rennie Mackintosh, and the building and its furniture and decor proved to be an outstanding example of his highly individual work.

Meanwhile, in 1896, the Association for the Promotion of Arts and Music ran out of money and the museum project was taken over by Glasgow Corporation. Some 62 plans were submitted for the design and Sir Alfred Waterhouse, the architect responsible for the Natural History Museum in London, chose the proposal from John W Simpson and E J Milner Allen. Work began promptly and the foundation stone was laid in September 1897.

THE PEOPLE'S PALACE

The following year saw the opening of another museum in the city on historic Glasgow Green. This area close to the river east and south of the cathedral has witnessed many dramatic episodes in the city's past. Indeed it owes its landscaping to public works aimed at alleviating the hardships of the unemployed in the period of the late 18th and early 19th centuries.

The People's Palace is a handsome red sandstone building with a dome and a conservatory (the Winter Gardens) at the back. Today it is the home of the city's social history collections and has displays reflecting both the work and leisure of Glasgow people. Mementoes of the once-popular music-halls, of footballers and other sporting heroes, can be seen alongside the grim reminders of city life during the Industrial Revolution and the inspiring records of those who tried to improve conditions for ordinary people.

Linked with the People's Palace today in the care of the District Council Museums Department, Provand's Lordship, the only surviving medieval dwelling house in the city (built in 1470), has displays reflecting the earlier years. Furniture from the 17th century is on show and one room is decorated as it would have been when the house was the home of the chaplain of the Hospital of St Nicholas.

ART GALLERY AND MUSEUM

By 1901 the new Art Gallery and Museum in Kelvingrove Park was ready. The handsome turreted exterior is of red Locharbriggs sandstone and the interior of white Giffnock stone. Some 20 display galleries are grouped around two glass-roofed side courts and a large central hall dominated by the great Lewis organ. The front entrance has an imposing portico above a sunken Italian garden. The back, looking up a tree-clad slope to Glasgow University, is approached by a double flight of steps and has a bronze statue of the city's patron saint, Mungo, or Kentigern, depicted appropriately as the protector of art and music.

In 1901 the park was transformed by elaborate landscaping projects including the diverting of the River Kelvin and by the building of numerous temporary pavilions for another Great International Exhibition of which the new gallery was the centrepiece. The summer was glorious and thousands of people enjoyed the colourful spectacle, visited the Japanese, Indian and Russian displays among others, and partook of refreshments at the numerous tea and coffee houses. Admission fees of one shilling (5p) for adults and sixpence (2½p) were charged.

The pavilions have disappeared but the Art Gallery (officially opened in 1902) remains as one of the most popular in Britain. The upper floors have displays of paintings from all the major European schools and are particularly rich in Dutch 17th-century art (including *The Man in Armour* by Rembrandt) and French painting of the Barbizon, Impressionist and Post-Impressionist periods (including *Going to Work* by Millet and *Blackfriars* by Derain). British painting of the 17th to 20th centuries is well represented with an emphasis on Scottish art, in particular the Glasgow Boys and Scottish Colourists.

There is at present no space to display all of the large and important collections of European glass, silver, jewellery and furniture, but selected items are shown along with the paintings of the appropriate periods; these are also displayed in the balcony area. A gallery on the ground floor is devoted to the work of Charles Rennie Mackintosh and his contemporaries who created the influential Glasgow Style.

For those particularly interested in Mackintosh, a short walk through Kelvingrove Park will bring them to the Hunterian Art Gallery of Glasgow University. There a suite of rooms by Mackintosh has been meticulously recreated adjoining the art gallery, whose outstanding collection of paintings by Whistler should not be missed.

Downstairs, the Art Gallery and Museum has a major display of European arms and armour, the highlights being the world-famous Milanese Gothic armour from Churburg, in northern Italy, and the English Greenwich armour for man and horse. Scottish weapons and militaria form an intriguing background to the armour exhibited here.

BURRELL
COLLECTION
*Powder-blue vase with
gilded fish, 17th- or 18th-
century, part of a collection
of Chinese ceramics; and
(below) European
medieval stained glass – the
Burrell has over 600 panels
of stained glass, ranging
from complete windows to
small roundels*

Other galleries have displays of Scottish prehistoric material and items illustrating the cultures of many different countries. the Natural History Department covers the zoology, geology and botany of the world.

POLLOK HOUSE
The opening of the Art Gallery and Museum in 1902 brought the number of civic galleries in the city to six. As well as the People's Palace there were small museums (now no longer in existence) at Camphill House, Tollcross House, Mosesfield and Aikenhead House. However, two names in the lists of organisers and contributors to the 1901 Exhibition catch the eye because of their promise of things to come. The names are those of the landowner, Sir John Stirling Maxwell, and the shipowner, Mr (later Sir) William Burrell.

The generous gift of Pollok House and 361 acres of gardens and parkland to the city in 1966 by Sir John's daughter, Mrs Anne Maxwell Macdonald, gave to the city its major surviving piece of 18th-century architecture. Sir John was responsible for the landscaping of the gardens we enjoy today, and in the house are displayed magnificent paintings collected by his father. These include major Spanish works by El Greco, Murillo and Goya. Some of the furnishings on view, such as the intricate astronomical clock, have been associated with the house for generations and in recent years have been augmented by 18th-century pieces with Scottish connections.

THE BURRELL COLLECTION
Turning to the other name, William Burrell, we find that he lent more than 200 items to the temporary exhibition in the Art Gallery. These included paintings by Manet, the Maris brothers and Joseph Crawhall, as well as glass, ivories, enamels, carpets and tapestries. Many of these objects are now on show in the Burrell Collection, which was opened to the public in Pollok Park in 1983.

In the years between 1901 and his death in 1958, William Burrell made two fortunes, received a knighthood and amassed one of the most astonishing collections ever owned by one man. He bought and renovated a castle near Berwick-upon-Tweed to be his home and the setting for his treasures. In 1944, after years of thought and consultation, he finally gifted the collection in the name of his wife and himself to Glasgow.

The Deed of Gift contained a number of stipulations, notably that certain large items of medieval stonework should be incorporated in the building in which the collection was to be displayed, that a number of the rooms at Hutton Castle should be recreated for display with their furniture and furnishings, and that the building should be at least six miles from the centre of Glasgow to preserve its contents from damage by pollution.

Finally all obstacles were overcome and an ideal site found in Pollok Park, thanks to the generosity of the Maxwell Macdonald family. The Clean Air Act and to a certain extent the decline of heavy industry in and around Glasgow have

TRANSPORT
Glasgow bade farewell to its trams in 1962, when they wound their way round in a last grand procession, but (left) this tramcar could still be admired in the old tramway depot, which was converted into a Museum of Transport. More recently Kelvin Hall has been renovated for an expanded Transport Museum

reduced atmospheric pollution, and the park proved to be an ideal setting for the award-winning new building designed by three young Cambridge architects, Barry Gasson, John Meunier and Brit Andreson.

This building, like the Art Gallery in Kelvingrove, is constructed of red Locharbriggs sandstone, but it has striking modern features like the dramatic glass wall looking out into the trees of Pollok Park. The Hutton rooms are grouped round a covered courtyard; the great Hornby Portal provides the entrance to the display gallery of items from the ancient civilisations, where the visitor can enjoy a rich variety of Egyptian, Assyrian, Greek and Roman objects.

There are Chinese ceramics, bronzes and jades, Japanese prints from the 18th and 19th centuries and, from the Near East, carpets and rugs, metalwork and ceramics. Sir William was particularly interested in European decorative arts and collected outstanding examples of medieval stained glass and tapestries, furniture, table glass, silver and needlework. Another of the great stone arches, from Montron in France, separates the sculpture gallery with its Rodin bronzes from the picture gallery where works by Degas, Manet, Cézanne, a Bellini *Virgin and Child* and a Rembrandt *Self-Portrait* are waiting to be enjoyed.

HAGGS CASTLE

A walk of 10 minutes or so separates the simple Palladian home of the Maxwells from the dramatic stone, timber and glass Burrell Collection building, but both are equally part of the rich heritage that Glasgow shares with its visitors. A short distance away stands a small much-restored castle, originally built for a branch of the Maxwell family in the 16th century.

Haggs Castle is now a museum for children. Here touching things is encouraged and children learn to appreciate history by dressing up and acting out scenes from the past. They pick herbs specially grown in the castle garden, make butter and learn simple weaving; they listen to music and learn the dances and the games of children of long ago.

THE TRANSPORT MUSEUM

Nearer in time and yet already a part of history are the City of Glasgow's famous tram cars. The first Museum of Transport was an old tramway depot, but the trams, the locomotives, the horse-drawn vehicles, the motor-cars and the world-famous ship models are being moved to a new and larger venue. In the spring of 1988, 100 years after the Great International Exhibition in Kelvingrove, the renovated Kelvin Hall, itself an exhibition venue for over 50 years will become the home of an expanded Transport Museum.

From the great art collections and the artefacts of the industries which funded the collections to the domestic bygones on show at the People's Palace and at the local history museums of Rutherglen and Springburn and the National Trust for Scotland's Tenement House, the range of Glasgow's museums and galleries is wide indeed, and genuinely provides something of interest for everyone.

Patricia Bascom is the Publications Officer of Glasgow Museums and Art Galleries.

HAGGS CASTLE
Mary Queen of Scots may well have visited Haggs Castle, which was certainly in existence at the time of the Battle of Langside. In 1987, 400 years after Mary's execution, children at Haggs helped to mark the anniversary, dressing up in splendid Tudor costumes. Haggs won the AA Best Museum for Scotland award in 1987

The Performing Arts

Glasgow's nomination as European City of Culture for 1990 is an international honour which it shares with Paris, Athens, Amsterdam, Florence and Berlin. The nomination comes as a surprise to people who do not know Glasgow, but to the generations of actors, musicians, singers, directors, designers, dancers and, most important of all, audiences, who have given and enjoyed some of the finest entertainment in Britain, it is just an international acknowledgement of the wealth of achievement in the visual and performing arts which have thrived in Glasgow for a very long time.

STRONG CHORAL TRADITION

There has always been music in Glasgow. Now more than ever it is impossible to be there and not be aware of the strong musical traditions which pervade the life of this bustling, energetic city.

The choral tradition in the central belt of Scotland is as strong as that of South Wales. Social hardship, the theory runs, drives people to seek beauty within their own society and choral singing is a natural result of this. Whatever the reason, Glasgow has had many fine choirs, the famous ones of the past including the Glasgow Orpheus Choir, the Glasgow Morriston Choir and the old Glasgow Choral Union, which is now the chorus of the Scottish National Orchestra, a magnificent international chorus. The city also boasts a bewildering array of amateur choral societies and small professional and semi-professional choruses, such as the Scottish Singers.

GLASGOW'S ORCHESTRAS

Glasgow has had its own orchestra since the 1890s—the Scottish Orchestra, which performed by royal command before Queen Victoria at Windsor in 1895. This orchestra played on a seasonal basis in the city under many distinguished conductors including John Barbirolli and George Szell, who both spent three years in Glasgow in the 1930s. Walter Susskind was its musical director in 1950 when it became the Scottish National Orchestra, a full-time orchestra with permanent 12-month contracts for its members. It was already an established and respected orchestra when, in 1959, the local-born conductor, Alexander Gibson, returned to Glasgow from London to become its conductor and music director. Since then the SNO has gone from strength to strength, making many distinguished foreign tours and fine recordings and performing regularly throughout Scotland. Gibson's successor, Neeme Jarvi, continues this fine tradition. The orchestra's old home, the St Andrew's Halls, was destroyed by fire in 1962 and never rebuilt as a concert hall, and for many years the SNO has performed regularly at the comparatively small City Hall in the centre of the city's old market area. But Glasgow is proud of its orchestra, and the plan to build a brand-new concert hall complex in time for the 1990 celebrations is just one of the many ways that the city celebrates its orchestral tradition.

The BBC also has a full-sized symphony orchestra based in Glasgow; it gives regular concerts in the city as well as having a busy schedule of broadcasts. The Scottish Chamber Orchestra too, although based in Edinburgh, gives as many concerts in Glasgow as it does in 'that other city' and, like the other two symphony orchestras, it has an enthusiastic and loyal following.

CHAMBER MUSIC

This wealth of orchestral activity provides a huge body of professional musicians in the city and they join up together to form every conceivable kind of chamber group. There are string quartets, wind ensembles and specialist groups (such as the Telemann Ensemble, which performs in Glasgow's biggest glasshouse, the Kibble Palace in the city's Botanic Gardens), all giving regular performances and all catering for every kind of musical taste.

Enthusiasts for early music are proud of the Scottish Early Music Consort, whose huge repertoire (all played on period instruments) includes an extremely bawdy collection of medieval ballads by the one-eyed Oswald von Wolkenstein as well as a justly popular programme of music from the time of Mary Queen of Scots.

Glasgow's concert halls, churches and theatres are obvious places to find music being performed. But the very popular chamber group, Cantilena, began when a handful of SNO musicians gathered to play Frescobaldi and Mozart together over a pint of beer in a city hotel. Now, a few years later, they have a string of successful recordings to their credit and an enormous public following in and out of Glasgow.

THE VARIOUS STAGES OF GLASGOW

Glasgow is still a city of theatres, despite the closing of the Alhambra, the Metropole, the Queen's, the Grand, the Empire and the Royalty. It has the King's Theatre, where local amateur companies (including the internationally renowned Glasgow Grand Opera Company, which once gave the British premières of Mozart's *Idomeneo* and Berlioz's *The Trojans*) share week-long seasons with shows fresh from the West End of London. It has the Pavilion, where the

PIPER
This Highlander is one player you are unlikely to hear in a Glasgow concert hall: the bagpipes sound their best in the open

BALLET
Opposite: the Scottish Ballet has won international acclaim for its repertoire of classical and modern works. Under its artistic director, Peter Darrell, the company tours extensively in Scotland and has had festival appearances throughout the world. In Glasgow, the company presents regular major productions at the Theatre Royal (here, Romeo and Juliet) and has opened its own Studio Theatre, Scotland's first custom-built venue for dance

ORCHESTRA
Scottish National Orchestra member plays the French horn

PERFORMING DOGS

Right: two playbills from the collection of the People's Palace. The one for the Queen's Theatre in 1852 promises an astonishing variety of drama, ballet, songs, farce . . . and performing dogs, and the one for the Pavilion in 1913 offers a rich assortment of music-hall entertainment

local comedians—successors to the legendary Harry Lauder and his contemporary heroes of the music-halls ('If you can play Glasgow, you can play *anywhere!*')—still command long runs to good and appreciative audiences. There is also the Citizens' Theatre with its enviable international reputation and its magnificent triumvirate of directors— Giles Havergal, Robert David MacDonald and Philip Prowse—where Shakespeare, Brecht, Karl Kraus, Beaumarchais, Goldoni, Albee, Balzac, Zola, O'Casey, Marlow, Pinter, Büchner, Wesker, Dryden, and Anon, meet

OPERA

This Scottish Opera production of Orlando *by Handel was first performed in May 1985. It was Scottish Opera's contribution to European Music Year, in celebration of Handel's bicentenary*

regularly to entertain the Citizens of Glasgow for not much more than than the price of a drink.

And then there is the Theatre Royal— described by one astounded reviewer, fresh off a train from the deep south, as 'the miracle at the top of Hope Street'. This is Scotland's only Opera House, bought by Scottish Opera after decades as a television studio and restored to its Victorian glory in browns and creams with brass gleaming like gold and seats so comfortable you could live in them. This is where Scottish Opera has its home, presenting performances which combine some of the world's finest singers with a wealth of Scottish talent. Alexander Gibson founded the company in 1962 and over the following quarter of a century it has delighted, astounded, dumbfounded and, occasionally, horrified audiences with opera productions to match the best in the world. Gibson's intention was to create an opera company worthy of its home city. He was knighted in the Queen's Jubilee Honours in 1977; the citation which accompanied his knighthood read simply 'for services to music in Scotland', six words which aptly describe a lifetime spent giving pleasure to millions. He also holds the St Mungo Award, given triennially by the Council to someone who has made Glasgow 'a better place to live'.

Since Scottish Opera is a touring company, the Theatre Royal is also home

to other performing companies. One of these is the Scottish Ballet, which has introduced the beauty of classical ballet and the excitement of modern dance to Glasgow. Like Scottish Opera, the ballet company operates an educational unit designed to produce young Glaswegians who will grow up not just enjoying the arts, but fully appreciating the dedicated performers who have provided them with such fine entertainment. Also in the Theatre Royal, the Scottish Theatre Company presents the finest Scottish actors to a true and very appreciative audience. Here too come regular visitors—the National Theatre, the Royal Shakespeare Company, Ballet Rambert, and many other theatre companies, dance companies and lighter entertainers.

There are other stages in Glasgow too. The adventurous Tron Theatre, in a converted church in the heart of old Glasgow, runs a popular programme of theatrical experiences for a mixed audience that is typical of Glasgow—blue rinse sits happily beside blue denim; short back and sides just along the row from Mohican punk.

Glasgow's theatre scene is also hot on social and political comment (but then, so were Mozart and Verdi, Beaumarchais and Shaw) and the city's arts festival, Mayfest, reflects this, mounting an annual programme which draws performing companies from all over the world. For all

of them, money and survival are two inseparable and perpetual problems. What better stimulus for the creative imagination? Glasgow's Mayfest is like the Edinburgh Fringe without Edinburgh's gentility; it is gutsy, unafraid and provocative—and Glaswegians love it.

'CINEMA CITY'

Although not a live performing art—at least not as far as its audiences are concerned—the cinema has played a vital part in the cultural development of Glasgow over the last 80 or so years. The picture house took over from the music-hall as the most popular form of entertainment in the early years of the 20th century, and the custom-built cinema very quickly became an architectural form in its own right. Glaswegians, despite their enthusiasm for music-hall, took to the new medium immediately, and between the two world wars Glasgow had over 130 cinemas—more 'silver screens' per head of population than any other city outside the United States. Glasgow also contained the largest picture theatre in Europe—the 4,400-seat Green's Playhouse, which operated as a cinema until 1973; it still exists, awaiting an uncertain fate. Another cinema still standing is the Vitagraph, at the Charing Cross end of Sauchiehall Street, easily recognisable by the enormous winged angel which stands above its pillared frontage.

Some of Glasgow's cinemas have disappeared; others have been converted into 'doubles' or 'triples'; others have, inevitably, changed their function in order to survive, becoming bingo halls; others lie derelict, sad survivors of a brief age of escapism, of impossible dreams, of glamour and of superstars. As architectural curiosities they are eminently 'collectable', and cinema spotters, who are as interested in the buildings themselves as in the transient celluloid images they once contained, can still have a field day in Glasgow's busy city centre and populous suburbs.

THE MUSIC OF THE STREETS

The art of performance in Glasgow is not just an indoor activity, for the city has its buskers and its street performers. There cannot be many cities in the world where shoppers are serenaded in the pedestrian precincts by accordion players giving them hour after hour of reels and strathspeys (with occasional audience participation!) or a kilted bagpiper playing stirring marches or sorrowful laments for long-dead Scottish heroes. Cinema queues in the city used to delight in the fairy music of the tin whistle, with tap dance accompaniment, provided by a gentleman of the road (and a hot favourite at university dances he was too), and it is

quite usual for music students from the Royal Scottish Academy to appear in summer sun to play duets, trios and quartets by Mozart, Beethoven, Brahms— or even Hamish McCunn!

THE FUTURE OF GLASGOW'S MUSIC

Glasgow has two universities and a distinguished Academy of Music and Drama. Between them these institutions secure the future of Glasgow's cultural reputation; the professional orchestras and the choruses in the city are enriched and sustained by the young talent which they supply, so that Glasgow's arts scene is vibrantly young and ambitious. Some artists move on quickly to make their mark in the wider world—Isobel Buchanan and Marie McLaughlin are just two young singers who have swept to international opera stardom within a year or two of leaving Glasgow. Others make their homes in the city and continue to provide a stable core for the arts that provide their living. It is this mixture of stability and flexibility which makes the performing arts in Glasgow so exciting.

The universities and the Academy also make music—much of it free—for the city: opera productions, plays, concerts, recitals and masterclasses are always available in the evenings or at lunchtimes, and Glaswegians, with an eye for a bargain as well as an ear for tomorrow's superstars, make the most of them.

It is comforting to know that Glasgow's cultural heritage is not just an accident of history; it is a deliberately planned and well-deserved reward for a long-term investment and it is well secured for the future. Even after 1990 has come and gone Glasgow will still be a great European City of Culture.

Roger Witts has worked as Director of Publicity for Scottish National Orchestra, the Edinburgh International Festival and, most recently, Scottish Opera.

EXPERIMENTS
At the doorway of the Tron Theatre, a popular experimental theatre in the Trongate, where Tron St Mary Church—a building with an eventful history— once stood

STREET ENTERTAINMENT
The pedestrian precinct of busy Argyle Street makes a stage for a group of buskers entertaining passers-by, and a more attentive audience, with their own celebration of Mayfest

Leaving aside saints, Glasgow has done quite well in throwing up larger-than-life characters who helped to shape its history.

BISHOP WISHART
Seal for the Chapter of the Cathedral of Glasgow, used in Wishart's episcopate. Bishop Wishart is particularly remembered for his part in the Scottish Wars of Independence

WILLIAM WALLACE
A pub sign in Elderslie, his birthplace. It was in Glasgow that Wallace was treacherously betrayed and captured in 1305

A BISHOP, A PROVOST AND A LASSIE

Among those who played an important role are several notable and usually very argumentative bishops, including Robert Wishart—'stout Robert Wishart'. Edward I of England, like so many English kings, had a psychotic urge to own Scotland, and tried to bribe this thrawn Scot to help him, but was indignantly turned down. Maybe the bribe wasn't big enough.

Wishart did offer allegiance to the same king when the puppet Scottish King Baliol collapsed, but soon threw his weight behind the liberator William Wallace, and was flung into jail when Wallace failed. It was Wishart who placed the Scottish crown on the head of Robert the Bruce, by which time the Bishop was old and blind. Overall, Wishart was a bit of a chancer, but when he was good he was very very good.

We shouldn't forget one of the earliest of the city's provosts, Thomas Crawford, whose life had more derring-do than the average civic leader's. Before he was appointed in 1577, he had served as one of Lord Darnley's 'young gentlemen' when that lacklustre individual married Mary Queen of Scots, and later was one of the commanders of the force that ended the five-year siege of Edinburgh Castle.

Perhaps his most notable single performance was his defiance of the Glasgow rabble which wanted to destroy the cathedral. He told them he was quite in favour, but not till they had built a new kirk in its place. He died in 1603, the year in which Darnley's son, James, became first monarch of the United Kingdom.

Regrettably this litany of the famous is very short of women, who doubtless ruled by stealth and didn't make the broadsheets. One of them does enter the list, however, almost by a back door, in the person of Frances Theresa, the stunningly beautiful daughter of Walter Stewart, third son of the Earl of Blantyre.

Stewart was a physician to Charles II, who was so besotted with the lady that he proposed to divorce his queen and marry the lassie. Shattered to learn that she was already secretly married to the Duke of Lennox, he nevertheless had her used as a model for Britannia and stamped on the backs of coins of the realm. So she lived on, ever beautiful, ever young—until decimalisation.

THE TOBACCO LORDS

The prodigious increase of the city's prosperity in the 18th century was attributed by the then Lord Provost very simply to just four talented and enthusiastic young men: William Cunninghame, Alexander Speirs, John Glassford and James Ritchie. They were the legendary Tobacco Lords. In their time, against fierce opposition from English seaports, the city's merchant fleet rose to 67; it carried manufactures to America and brought back tobacco and mountains of money. Glassford alone had 25 busy vessels. All four of the men bought huge estates and lived, indeed, like lords.

And they didn't disguise their success. They became virtually a tourist attraction as they paraded on the plainstanes in the Trongate decked out in scarlet cloaks, powdered wigs, silken hose and buckled shoes. When they strolled, lesser mortals cleared off the plainstanes to make way for them.

They had a mighty fall with the American War of Independence. But the memory lingers on.

DAVID DALE, COTTON KING AND IDEALIST

People who have totally forgotten the Tobacco Lords in Glasgow still remember David Dale. He was a wee Ayrshire boy herding cows till he came to the big city and made a fortune as a linen merchant. But he had a passionate wish for the rights of the workers. He decided to go into cotton, and attracted such geniuses as the Lancashire weaver, James Hargreaves, with his spinning jenny, Richard Arkwright, a barber who designed a new kind of loom, and Samuel Crompton, improbably a clergyman, who put other inventions together to produce the mule, a machine that leapt stubbornly ahead of the technology of the time.

Dale founded the cotton mills of New Lanark and launched his ideal society in which the workers must have their rights. The rights were, of course, specified by Dale and not by the workers. It was a time of magical perfectionism, and his son-in-law, Robert Owen, joined him to create the ideal society.

The mills worked quite well. The ideal society did not. The mills have been preserved and are worth seeing. They don't look like the kind of suburb most of us would like to live in. A matter of individual taste of course.

JAMES WATT, INVENTOR OF THE INDUSTRIAL REVOLUTION

James Watt was born in Greenock. Legend has it that he once sat in his mother's kitchen watching a kettle boiling on the hob, held a spoon to the spout and saw the spoon being pushed by the steam. This is an entertaining piece of historical rubbish. Steam from a spout cannot push

anything.

What is reasonably true is that Watt got a job at Glasgow University as a humble mechanic, was required to do routine repairs on such things as a Newcomen steam-engine and realised that the thing was vastly inefficient. Watt didn't invent the steam-engine. He made it ten times better. He did initiate the Industrial Revolution, because his steam-engine was the motive force of that wild experience.

Watt was an incurable inventor. He constructed organs, he mended fiddles, he created the first duplicating machine, a letterpress still quite common in offices until the 1930s. It is ironic that he would never have done any of this without the passionate interest of an Englishman, Matthew Boulton, who whisked him away from Glasgow to the English Midlands and made the dreamer's dreams come true.

HENRY BELL, ENTREPRENEUR
After James Watt, as every Scottish schoolchild used to know, came Henry Bell, who invented the steamship. This is nonsense. Bell invented nothing. He merely hired a man to build a ship and another man to install a steam-engine in it. He was an entrepreneur and nothing else.

William Symington was way ahead of Bell, with a steamship that plied briefly on the Forth and Clyde Canal. It was called the *Charlotte Dundas*, and it was fine, except that its wash destroyed the canal banks. It did inspire the American, Robert Fulton, to build the steamer *Clermont*, which plied between New York and Albany.

In other words, Henry Bell was not what we thought he was. But he was very good at getting the headlines and he is remembered when the others are forgotten. Glasgow is quite proud of him.

TOBACCO LORD
Distinguished by scarlet cloak and gold-headed cane

JAMES WATT
The man who made steam power efficient

JAMES MAXTON
*In 1922, Maxton (right)
was elected to the House of
Commons, one of 10
members of the Independent
Labour Party who gained
seats that year to represent
Glasgow. Known as the
Clydesiders, this group had
an aggressive style which
often upset more
conventional fellow MPs,
but Maxton's irresistible
charm won him enormous
popularity*

JOHN ANDERSON, MAN OF MANY PARTS

One of the formative influences on the life of James Watt was a man whose name has made a permanent mark on Glasgow's map. It was John Anderson, professor of natural philosophy (or science, if you like), who took the young inventor under his wing and made his library and apparatus available to him.

An all-round man, Anderson. In 1745, as a boy in Stirling, he had raised a regiment to defend the town against Prince Charles's warriors. He planned the fortifications of Greenock to ward off a possible attack from the French. He invented a recoilless field gun, which was pooh-poohed by the British Government; so he sold it to France.

France, in the process of exporting the French Revolution, wanted its brilliant ideas known all over Europe but couldn't get past the German frontier. Anderson created a flight of paper balloons filled with hot air to carry the French propaganda across the frontier.

This, we can assume, was only a bit of fun for the man. He was passionately in favour of extending education to working men, and to women, and organised lectures for them. When he died, his entire estate went to the foundation of a college for all classes and both sexes—the first technical college in the world.

JOHN ALEXANDER MACDONALD, GLASGOW'S SPIRITED EXPORT

John Alexander MacDonald's name is not too big in his native city because, like many other Glaswegians, he made his mark far away from home. In 1820, when the lad was five, his parents emigrated to Canada to escape hard times. It was a good move. He worked hard at his studies and was called to the Bar at the age of 25, plunged into politics and was leader of the Conservatives 20 years later.

His prime achievement was to weld the provinces into the Dominion of Canada. His career had a few hiccups—this is true in both senses, because John A was fond of his dram, and it sometimes showed when he was addressing Parliament. But as another Member said, he would rather listen to John drunk than most other speakers sober. There was also a wee whiff of sharp practice when he was organising the railways across the new country.

But he survived all that, and was in power from 1878 until his death in 1891. If Glasgow doesn't know much about him, he is still a tall legend in Canada.

MADELEINE SMITH— MURDERESS?

People still write plays and essays and bits of self-indulgence about Madeleine Smith. She was charged with murder. At the High Court in Edinburgh, she was not actually acquitted. The jury's verdict was 'not proven', a peculiar Scottish phenomenon which suggests that the jury was pretty sure she did it but that the evidence wasn't enough for a verdict of guilty.

Madeleine was the daughter of a successful Glasgow architect, one of whose creations, the McLellan Galleries in Sauchiehall Street, is still to be seen and enjoyed. In 1855 she met a penurious Channel Islander, Pierre Emil L'Angelier, and had a passionate love affair with him.

She lived at 7 Blythswood Square, and now and then the mad young L'Angelier would crouch in the area and be fed endearments and cocoa. He died of arsenic poisoning. This was shortly after Madeleine had met a very marriageable young man, William Kinnoch. Did she feed Pierre the arsenic? She had certainly bought some, apparently for use in the family garden on the Firth of Clyde.

We can't tell. She got off. She moved to London, married and was a social success. She moved to America and everybody loved her. A film producer asked her to play her young self in a reconstruction of the drama. She refused. She was over 90 when she died, and she had never told anybody what really happened. She had style. Guilt? We will never know.

JAMES MAXTON, THE 'BELOVED REBEL'

Glasgow has always been a nurse of rebels. Keir Hardie, the founder of the Labour Party, was born in Lanarkshire, worked his anger out in Ayrshire, and was the first Labour MP elected to Parliament—for West Ham.

Among the host of fierce workers for the equality of the classes, probably the most endearing and the most remembered is James Maxton. When he was the Member for Bridgeton, for the Independent Labour Party, it was said that the polling officials didn't count his votes, they just weighed them.

Maxton was born into a comfortable middle-class family in 1885, in the suburb of Barrhead, took a very Conservative view of society through his university career, and then suddenly turned against the inequalities of society. He went to prison as a pacifist in the First World War and spent his time trying to convert his Edinburgh prison officers to pacifism.

The Labour movement split up during his time in Parliament. Maxton stuck to the old Independent Labour Party and led it. In political terms he led it into the wilderness, but he was a man whom everybody loved. An orator of passion and humour, he was always his own man. Although in theory totally against British institutions, he was a great parliamentarian. When he tangled with Winston Churchill during the Second World War, it was with mutual respect.

His biographer, John McNair, called him the Beloved Rebel. He is remembered because he was not concerned with power but with justice and affection. There are worse roads to fame.

CHARLES RENNIE MACKINTOSH

Glasgow School of Art is now a place of pilgrimage for visitors from all over the world. They just like to look at it, outside and inside.

It is certainly the major creation of the architect, Charles Rennie Mackintosh, who was born in Glasgow in 1868 and had a pretty hard time. His work (apart from the School of Art) was always more admired by foreigners than by his fellow countrymen, and he never had any success in financial terms. It has taken decades since his death in 1929 for the Mackintosh cult to get off the ground, but he has been one of the great names in the development of ideas in the city.

His furniture designs are now being reproduced by an Italian company and are fetching ludicrous prices. His dining chairs are spectacular to look at; few people would actually want to sit on them.

Mackintosh was a prime specimen of the prophet who is not without honour except in his own country. There is now a thriving Mackintosh Centre at Queen's Cross in Garscube Road, where admirers pay a belated tribute to a man of stubborn genius.

TOM HONEYMAN AND HIS DALI

Another rebel, and a beloved and comfortable rebel, totally Glaswegian and totally international, was Doctor Tom Honeyman. Born in 1891, Tom was in fact a doctor of medicine, but although he was very good at it, his passion was art. After working with an art gallery company, he became Glasgow's Director of Art Galleries and Museums in 1939.

What he is remembered for, and not unfairly, is his bold decision in 1952 to use a discretionary fund to buy Dali's *Christ of St John of the Cross*. He squandered £8,200 on his whim. Many of the city councillors, his employers, went livid at the extravagance. Tom introduced a novelty to the operation of the Kelvingrove Park galleries, a small charge for admission to the Dali room. Citizens queued round the building in thousands, thus writing off the extravagance in a few weeks. Reproductions of the picture have brought to the galleries copyright fees which are cautiously not revealed to the public. The picture is probably worth an amount running into seven figures today.

The city council's angry response to Doctor Honeyman's act of defiance was to change the department's name to the Museums and Art Galleries Department. He resigned in 1954. His name outlives those of the cautious men who were appalled by his reckless use of public money.

JAMES BRIDIE AND THE GLASGOW CITIZENS' THEATRE

A contemporary and lifelong friend of Tom Honeyman was James Bridie. Born Osborne Henry Mavor (Scots have a curious passion for pseudonyms) Bridie was also a doctor of medicine—a notable consultant, who suddenly developed a passion for the theatre. His first play was produced by the Scottish National Players in 1928: *Sunlight Sonata*, it was called, and its author, 'Mary Henderson'.

From there he went on, as Bridie, to write a stream of plays: *The Anatomist, A Sleeping Clergyman, Mr Bolfry, Dr Angelus, Daphne Laureola* and others. Many of them were more appreciated outside of Scotland than in his native city. 'Twas ever thus.

Bridie was the creator, with friends like Honeyman, of the Glasgow Citizens' Theatre, designed to provide a stage for Scottish writing and acting. The theatre has long abandoned this purpose—but it is still a theatre; James Bridie has not lived entirely in vain. He was one of the most amiable men ever produced by Glasgow and possessed an intellect which was overshadowed by his sheer niceness.

JAMES BRIDIE
A drawing by Mervyn Peake shows James Bridie in 1939, aged 51. Himself a doctor, Bridie must have been fascinated by Dr Pritchard, the subject of his play Dr Angelus. *An autobiography,* One Way of Living, *describes Bridie's life in Glasgow in the 20s and 30s. Top: the theatre he helped create. It moved in 1945 to the Gorbals*

JOURNALISTIC CELEBRATIONS OF GLASGOW

If the journalist is a lowly form of life, Glasgow has produced some of the greatest of these lowly, including Hugh Foulis, who as Neil Munro wrote good novels and the magical tales of *Para Handy* (which were produced for the *Glasgow Evening News* when he was its editor, and which he rather despised).

There was Harold Stewart, who appeared in the *Daily Record* as the Gangrel, writing a daily comic column superior to most of the work in London and New York.

There was, and is, Jack House, now into his eighties and still pouring out words about the city with which he is besotted. He has worked for most Glasgow newspapers during his very long life as a scribbler, and has produced a list of books which celebrate the city as a centre of fun, and murder, and nonsense.

It is easy to dismiss the journalist as a man whose words are written on the wind. House is not to be dismissed, nor is his contribution. What he has done is to give Glaswegians a sense of identity. This is the kind of man who creates a reality which was unnoticed before he opened the city's eyes to it. He is famous, and rightly so.

BILLY CONNOLLY

Statesmen, philosophers, inventors, entrepreneurs, the Glaswegian takes with quiet pride. But the supreme product of the city is its humour, and the people it has really taken to its heart are its laughter-makers. Many have been so intensely Glaswegian that their magic has been incomprehensible to outsiders, and it is really astonishing that one of the most intense of all can now perform to enchanted audiences in England and North America.

Billy Connolly served his apprenticeship in the shipyards, cracked jokes and moonlighted as a folk singer. When he decided to go full-time as an entertainer with the Humblebums folk group, his father was really worried about the abandonment of a steady trade.

Looking at the Clyde shipyards today we can see that's pretty funny in itself.

He branched out on his own, as a folk singer. Like some others, he began to find that the bits of chat between the songs — the inconsequential patter that gives a man time to tune the instrument — was getting more response than the songs.

He still sings, but the patter is the real matter. It is quite outrageous, it explores the cruder side of human experience but with a marvellous innocent delight. His manic energy communicates his own delighted wonder at the daftness of life and offers a catharsis to quite well-bred foreigners.

He himself will read this with some misgivings, because he's convinced that any attempt to analyse humour must end up destroying the joke. He needn't worry. Billy is indestructible.

Cliff Hanley

thrawn: *stubborn*

plainstanes: *central pavement, boulevard*

KENNY DALGLISH, FOOTBALL HERO

As a fitba'-crazy city, Glasgow has thrown up a whole pantheon of soccer heroes, and among the contemporary players racing in the footsteps of the legendary Jimmy McGrory is Kenny Dalglish. He started as a junior with Cumbernauld United and was snapped up, still in his teens, by Glasgow Celtic to play in their historic victory in the European Cup in 1967 — the first British team ever to take that honour.

In the following year he transferred to Liverpool as a player, and demonstrated not only skill and power, but the other thing that can't be learned — star quality. Just after the Heysel Stadium disaster in 1985 he became player-manager at Liverpool and, still in his thirties continued to dazzle the crowds.

CITY CENTRE

*The reflection of St George's Tron Church in a modern
building succinctly expresses the exciting diversity that
characterises Glasgow's architecture*

Argyll Arcade, with its light and airy, glazed hammerbeam roof, is a most civilised place to shop for jewellery

ANNAN GALLERY

West Campbell Street
Still run by the family who established it in 1855, this is a traditional art gallery which deals in original paintings by Scottish and Continental artists, as well as a wide range of prints of Scottish scenes. But it is particularly well known for its unique collection of historic Glasgow photographs, many on Victorian glass negatives, which have been used to illustrate books and magazine articles about the city.

In a collection of more than 500 negatives—prints of which are always available—there are especially good sections on old Clyde steamers and Glasgow trams, notable city buildings and long-vanished closes, and the three Great Exhibitions of 1888, 1901 and 1911 in Kelvingrove Park.

ARGYLL ARCADE

Argyle Street and Buchanan Street
Built in 1827, this is Glasgow's original glass-roofed shopping arcade, running from Argyle Street to Buchanan Street, with a right-angled bend in the middle.

Towards the end of the 18th century, Buchanan Street was the western edge of the city, where wealthy merchants lived in some style. Where the arcade now stands there was a fashionable coffee house, and a courtyard in which wagers of up to 1,000 guineas were made on cockfights.

As the population of the city grew, there was money to be made in providing new shopping facilities. The building of the Argyll Arcade was financed by John Reid, a well-to-do timber importer. The present-day Sloan's Restaurant, on the site of the old coffee house, retains Reid's splendid mahogany staircases.

Below the high and airy glass canopy of the arcade, in shops whose fascias are decorated with the badges of famous Scottish clans and families, more than 20 goldsmiths, silversmiths, diamond merchants and jewellers go about their business.

THE BARROWS (THE BARRAS)

Gallowgate and London Road
The biggest indoor market in Scotland—scattered around individual buildings where stalls stock antiques and collectors' items, second-hand clothes, shoes, furniture, soft furnishings, glassware, electrical goods, carpets, linoleum, stationery, brass, records and take-away food—is an updating of the legendary 'Barras' where poor folk from the East End of Glasgow used to make a meagre living as street traders.

The person who made the best living from the trade was Maggie Maciver. She had a fleet of 300 barrows for hiring out to the traders, and in the 1920s built a covered-in market for them in this network of little streets east of Glasgow Cross.

Although the barrows themselves have mostly gone, this remains a place of weekend bustle and non-stop patter from the more energetic stallholders. The goods on sale are much more respectable than they sometimes were in the old days— · men's suits which turned out, when unwrapped at the customer's home, to have been cut for somebody with only one leg; or perfume which was actually watered-down disinfectant.

BELLAHOUSTON PARK

Bellahouston Drive, Dumbreck Road and Mosspark Boulevard
Featuring lawns which sweep up to a wooded viewpoint ridge, this park was the site of the great Empire Exhibition of 1938. Very few traces of the exhibition remain, although the Palace of Art, now outside the park boundary, is still used as an education centre. The Palace of Engineering was taken to pieces and reassembled as a factory at Prestwick Airport.

There are football pitches and a jogging track, and an indoor sports centre with facilities for everything from netball to judo. Many business people come along for a session of lunchtime squash.

The Glasgow Ski Centre offers lessons—for six-year-olds upwards—on a small artificial slope. And in June rally cars usually tackle a route over the tarmac driveways as a high-speed stage in the International Scottish Rally.

BLYTHSWOOD SQUARE

This elegant hilltop square is one of the city's prestige business addresses, favoured by banking, finance and investment houses, civil engineers, advertising and marketing firms. The whole east side is occupied by the clubhouse of the Royal Scottish Automobile Club; the starting-ramp for the International Scottish Rally in June is usually outside the main entrance, just as this used to be the British starting-point for the Monte Carlo Rally.

The fine buildings of the square, dating from the 1820s and many times renovated, look onto private gardens. A few years ago there was a ludicrous proposal, successfully fought off, to have the gardens turned into a car park.

Charlie Rennie Mackintosh designed the doorway of Number 5 for the Glasgow Society of Lady Artists, whose headquarters used to be here.

Number 7 was the home of Madeleine Smith, the defendant in one of Scotland's most famous murder trials. In 1857 she was accused of poisoning her lover, Emile l'Angelier. The case causes considerable discussion even today, largely because of the compromise Scottish verdict of 'not proven' brought in by the jury. This is usually taken to mean 'go away and don't do it again!'

In the Barrows, stalls have largely replaced the original 'barras', but the atmosphere of this lively weekend market is still thick with sales patter and bargain hunters

The Botanic Gardens were opened to the public in 1891, 50 years after moving to their present site from Sauchiehall Street. The 42 acres include specialised gardens and two ranges of glasshouses

BOTANIC GARDENS

Great Western Road
Glasgow's original Botanic Gardens, themselves the successors to an even older university Physic Garden, were menaced by the westward expansion of the city in early Victorian times. In 1842 a second and so far final move was made to this site, which seems from the main road to be on a gentle slope, but actually dips sharply on its northern edge to include the very pleasant wooded valley of the River Kelvin, crossed by footbridges.

The most notable building in the gardens is the Kibble Palace. Its domed and interlinked circular glasshouses are based on a conservatory which originally stood in the grounds of John Kibble's Coulport House on Loch Long. He was a mildly eccentric engineer, one of whose inventions was a bicycle on floats, which he pedalled along the loch.

The Kibble Palace covers an area of 23,000 square feet (2137 sq m), and is one of the largest as well as one of the most spectacular glasshouses in Britain. It contains a splendid collection of soaring tree ferns from Australia and New Zealand, and plants from Africa, North and South America and the Far East. There are exhibition wings, and the main dome also houses a number of Victorian sculptures which fit in remarkably well with their exotic surroundings.

More conventional in design, the Main Range of glasshouses includes 11 linked buildings, each with a particular speciality: orchids, for instance, tropical flowers, aquatics and the British national collection of begonias.

Below: spectacular domed top of the Kibble Palace, erected in the Botanic Gardens in 1873

Left: a white marble Victorian nymph admires her surroundings in the Kibble Palace

The grounds are laid out with lawns and conventional flowerbeds. But although the founders—the Royal Botanic Institution of Glasgow—passed on control of the gardens to Glasgow Corporation as long ago as 1891, and they are now one of the city's public parks, their basic function has not been forgotten. A number of 'theme' plots complement the study and display facilities under glass.

BRIGGAIT CENTRE

Clyde Street and Bridgegate
Running from Glasgow Cross to what was first a ford and then a bridge over the Clyde, the Bridgegate existed as early as 1124. Fishermen's cottages once stood here, so it was an appropriate location in the 1870s for the city's ornate fishmarket.

That market moved elsewhere; but the Victorian building has found a new lease of life as the Briggait Centre, a tall indoor shopping mall with a glass roof, fine ironwork and a first-floor gallery. There are food and dress shops, paintings and jewellery, a restaurant and bar, music and regular busking sessions.

Leading from the courtyard to the North Gallery of the Burrell Collection, the 16th-century Hornby Castle Portal is among several fine features that are incorporated in the building's fabric

BURRELL COLLECTION/ POLLOK COUNTRY PARK

Pollokshaws Road
In his introduction to the Burrell Collection guidebook, John Julius Norwich puts the matter very plainly: 'In all history, no municipality has ever received from one of its native sons a gift of such munificence.' But the phenomenal art collection presented to Glasgow in 1944 by the millionaire shipowner Sir William Burrell and his wife is only one of the outstandingly generous gifts which make up Pollok Country Park.

The 361 acres of the park were presented to the city in 1966 by Mrs Anne Maxwell Macdonald, whose family owned the extensive Pollok estates for almost 700 years; and her gift included the elegant Palladian mansion of Pollok House.

Although Victorian Glasgow was accustomed to lavish endowments from its wealthier citizens, no city in recent times has seen anything to match this generosity.

The Burrell Collection was gathered together over something like 80 years. Sir William was born in 1861, entered the family shipping company of Burrell and Son in 1876, virtually retired from business during the First World War, and was still collecting, valuing and dealing with agents until shortly before his death in 1958.

He collected widely but within certain well-defined areas of personal interest; he was well informed, had generally excellent taste and a shrewd appreciation of values, and, without ever overspending, he was able to amass a collection unmatched by rivals far wealthier than himself. Enthusiasts for 'the Burrell' are instantly resentful of the suggestion that he was any kind of 'magpie'.

As it is seen in the modern gallery specially built for it in 1983, the Burrell Collection includes individual sections which range from Ancient Egyptian stonework, Greek and Italian earthenware; magnificent ceramics and bronzes from Persia and China; Japanese prints; carpets, tapestries, religious figurines, silver and glassware, furniture and furnishings, stained glass and needlework . . . to 17th-century Dutch portraits by Rembrandt and Frans Hals, and a number of French paintings by Boudin, Sisley, Manet, Degas and Cézanne.

Medieval portals and windows are set in the walls of warm

The Thinker, probably Auguste Rodin's best-known work, is one of 14 bronzes by this sculptor in the Burrell Collection

Dumfriesshire sandstone. Some of the stained-glass collection is displayed against outer windows facing the afternoon sun; and, emphasising the gallery's country-in-the-city location, one long glass wall looks directly out onto woodlands which change their colours as the seasons progress.

Visitors come back time and again to the Burrell. After the first stunned look round, they return to admire particular favourite pieces: a delicate Korean bowl, perhaps, about 800 years old and valued at a quarter of a million pounds; some splendid medieval wood-carving; or Alfred Sisley's glorious autumn painting *The Bell Tower at Noisy-le-Roi*.

From time to time the displays are discreetly altered because, of the 8,000 items in the collection, there is room for only 3,000 to be shown.

The inner courtyard of the gallery forms a striking introduction. In the centre, surrounded by fig trees, stands the massive Warwick Vase, rebuilt from fragments of the original found on the site of the Emperor Hadrian's villa at Tivoli near Rome, a classical ideal for 18th- and 19th-century trophies.

Round three sides of the courtyard the principal rooms of Sir William Burrell's home at Hutton Castle in Berwickshire have been reconstructed, because this remarkable and publicity-shunning man, whose picture—on his own specific instructions—is nowhere to be seen in the gallery, continued with his gifts to Glasgow even after his death.

Like the Burrell Collection, Pollok House is open to visitors free of charge. The mansion house looks out over elevated gardens to the valley of the White Cart Water.

Curiously enough, there is no certainty about who designed the central and original part of Pollok House in the middle of the 18th century, because all the documents relating to the building of it have been lost. Mrs Maxwell Macdonald's gift in 1966 included furniture, ceramics, silver and glassware which had been in the family for generations, as well as part of the finest privately owned collection of Spanish paintings in Britain—works by Goya, Murillo and El Greco.

Pollok Country Park features a Demonstration Garden where amateurs are given advice on subjects as varied as fertilisers, dahlias and window-boxes.

An interpretation centre provides information on riverside and woodland trails, the wildlife of the park—including its 10 species of butterflies—and the history of the estate. A Young Naturalists' Club arranges outdoor and indoor activities, and for a different age group there is also a 50+ Club.

Perhaps the aristocrats of the park are the Pollok fold (or herd) of Highland cattle. These splendid shaggy beasts, with traditional Gaelic names, represent the City of Glasgow at agricultural shows all over the country.

It is another sign of the remarkable variety at Pollok that a place which displays alabaster ware created by artists of the Old Kingdom of Egypt 4,500 years ago, medieval German tapestries and a Rembrandt self-portrait, is also the stamping ground of Supreme Champions like Angus Og of Glenogle and Cailleach Bheag.

The imposing Warwick Vase stands proudly in the inner courtyard of the Burrell

In Pollok Park, a view over the White Cart Water shows the stately Pollok House. Treasures on view in the house include an exceptional collection of Spanish paintings – by artists such as El Greco, Murillo and Goya – and six paintings by Blake

The Parish Church of Carmunnock, a village striving to preserve its identity within the boundaries of Glasgow

CARMUNNOCK

Although it was taken within the Glasgow boundaries in 1938, this is a separate village entirely out of sight of the city, in a fold of the hills on its southern edge. A religious community was established here in the 6th century, and the parish church—rebuilt in its present form in 1767—is the focal point of the village, set in a maze of central lanes. Outside stairways lead to the church's upper galleries, and at ground-floor level there is the burial vault—kept remarkably dry by its thick marble-lined walls—of the Stewarts of Castlemilk. They were the landed family here for many generations, but their estate is now largely given over to one of Glasgow's post-war council housing schemes.

The parishioners of Carmunnock were very worried at the time of the 19th-century 'resurrectionists' who exhumed newly buried corpses for sale to the city's anatomy schools. In 1828 a watch-house was built inside the churchyard gate. It is still kept in good repair, like the painted set of Regulations for the Watch, with their stern prohibitions on drinking while on duty and unnecessary firing-off of guns.

Some 18th-century houses survive near the church. When these were built, many local families made their living from hand-loom weaving. Once that cottage industry was killed off by competition from the larger mills, the people turned to laundry work. Until well into this century, carts would leave Carmunnock every Wednesday morning with freshly laundered clothes and linen to be delivered to regular customers in the city; in the afternoon they would toil back up the hill with the next week's wash.

Present-day Carmunnock fights hard to retain its village atmosphere. It has an active Preservation Society, a variety of local clubs and societies, a Gala Week and annual Highland Games.

CHARLES RENNIE MACKINTOSH CENTRE

Queen's Cross Church, Garscube Road
This is a notable building—the only church designed by Glasgow's most famous architect, Charles Rennie Mackintosh. Completed in 1899, it is a curious but forceful combination of his Art Nouveau approach with a much older medieval tradition. There are traces of Gothic Revival, but the carvings and decorative details in wood and stone are strictly Art Nouveau.

In 1976 the congregation of Queen's Cross moved to another church nearby. Four years later, the Charles Rennie Mackintosh Society took over a lease of the building. The Society, which has more than 1,500 members all over the world—some as far away as Japan—began a long programme of restoration work.

This is also the Society's headquarters, with facilities for lectures and exhibitions, and a comprehensive reference library. It has a tea room and a well-stocked shop which concentrates on all manner of items using Mackintosh designs, including prints which are a vivid reminder that in the 1920s, after his architectural practice had faded, he lived in the south of France and painted some very fine watercolours.

Clearly Mackintosh's priority in his design of this high-back chair was not comfort. The Charles Rennie Mackintosh Centre provides some insights into the aims and achievements of this highly original architect, designer and painter

CITIZENS' THEATRE

Gorbals Street
Dating from 1878, and known originally as the Royal Princess's Theatre, this is the only surviving building in an otherwise demolished block in the once-notorious Gorbals district of the city. Just after the pantomime season of 1944–5, the owner leased it at a minimum rent to the Glasgow Citizens' Theatre, formed by the playwright James Bridie.

The present repertory company was founded in 1970, but it keeps an old Royal Princess's tradition alive. Although its main performances are of plays such as Sheridan's *School for Scandal*, Miller's *Death of a Salesman* and Pinter's *No Man's Land*, the same actors turn their hand every December and January to a children's pantomime.

Now the headquarters of Glasgow District Council, the City Chambers building is a proud expression of Victorian confidence and prosperity

The Forth and Clyde Canal, once an important thoroughfare, now enjoys the prospect of extensive revitalisation as a historic waterway and recreation area

CITY CHAMBERS

George Square
Guided tours of this magnificent building on the east side of George Square show more clearly than anything else in the city the opulence of Glasgow in its Victorian heyday.

The entrance hall has the floor plan of a Renaissance-style Roman church, with granite columns topped by marble capitals. Its vaulted ceiling is decorated with one and a half million Venetian mosaic cubes.

A very grand marble and alabaster staircase—deliberately undecorated so as to show off the beauty of the polished stone—leads to the sumptuous Banqueting Hall and the semicircular Council Hall with its mahogany and tapestry-lined walls. In the smaller Satinwood Salon, the amberwood-panelled Octagonal Room and the Mahogany Salon, paintings are on loan from the finest municipal art collection in Britain.

CITY HALL

Candleriggs
When St Andrew's Halls were gutted by fire in 1962, Glasgow lost its principal venue for choir and orchestral concerts. A new concert hall at the top of Buchanan Street should be ready by 1990. In the interval, the old City Hall was brought back into service for prestige events like the regular concert series of the Scottish National Orchestra.

Older Glaswegians still talk of much less dignified proceedings in the City Hall: the 'Bursts' were music-hall entertainments whose organisers unwisely provided the audience with paper bags containing snacks. Inevitably, once the bags were empty, they were blown up and exploded—regardless of what emotional or dramatic moment had been reached on stage.

CROOKSTON CASTLE

Towerside Crescent
On a lightly wooded hilltop, with a view beyond the city to the Renfrewshire moors, this is the only castle in Glasgow classified as an Ancient Monument. In 1931, it became the first property of the National Trust for Scotland.

The Stewarts of Darnley built the present castle in the 15th century, on the site of a wooden fortress dating from the time of Robert Croc—who gave his name to Crookston—around 1180. Croc's circular defensive ditch is still crossed to reach the castle.

Henry, Lord Darnley, was the almost entirely inadequate husband of Mary, Queen of Scots. The couple spent some time at Crookston in 1567 before moving to Edinburgh, where Darnley was murdered, probably on the instructions of the Earl of Bothwell, who then replaced him as the Queen's much sturdier consort.

FORTH AND CLYDE CANAL

An ambitious scheme has been started to revitalise this historic waterway, which wanders through the north-west suburbs and also has a branch finishing near the city centre. The plan is to remove obstacles, rebuild bridges and reopen the canal to navigation for the first time since 1963.

A cruise boat will operate northwards from Maryhill, canalside pubs and restaurants will be encouraged, picnic and parking areas provided, and the canal's impressive wealth of industrial archaeology exploited.

Already, the towpath near the canal offices in Applecross Street provides good traffic-free walking, with fine views across the city to the stately towers of the Park Conservation Area.

GEORGE SQUARE

This is the principal square in the city, with colourful flowerbeds surrounding the Cenotaph and a collection of 12 statues. Unusually for the west of Scotland, Sir Walter Scott occupies the most elevated position, on top of a towering pillar, while Robert Burns plays a supporting role.

Also commemorated is Colin Campbell, Lord Clyde. His 93rd Highlanders were 'the thin red line' at Balaclava, and he also commanded the relief force at Lucknow. His boyhood home was just a few minutes' stroll away in John Street, one block east.

Sir Walter Scott, poet and novelist – the dominating statue in George Square

GLASGOW CATHEDRAL

Cathedral Square

Long before Glasgow existed, there was a place called Cathures on the banks of the Molendinar Burn in the kingdom of Strathclyde. In the 5th century, St Ninian came here from Galloway to dedicate a Christian burial ground. A few generations later, St Kentigern arrived in a burial party, eventually settled here and was elected bishop by popular acclaim.

Kentigern means 'Chief Lord', but the well-loved Bishop was known more usually as Mungo—'Dear One'. This is why the place in

Glasgow Cathedral, a fine example of Gothic architecture and Glasgow's oldest building

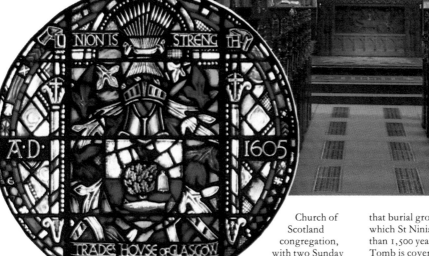

Detail of a window in the cathedral, one of the many that have been renewed recently in modern stained glass depicting various city motifs

the cathedral where he was buried—according to tradition on 13 January 603—is called St Kentigern's Tomb, but it is as St Mungo that he features as the city's patron saint.

The cathedral was started in the 12th century and completed about 300 years later. It was menaced at the angry time of the Reformation; but the trade guilds of Glasgow and supporters from the neighbouring royal burgh of Rutherglen formed an armed guard on it, and very little damage was done.

The lofty nave and choir, forming the upper church, are on the main entrance level. The cathedral has a Church of Scotland congregation, with two Sunday services and one on Wednesday mornings.

In the choir, the pews are named after city organisations that helped with their renovation in 1957, and with the protection of the cathedral at other times: for example, the Institute of Chartered Accountants in Scotland, Glasgow School of Art and the Clyde Navigation Trust, and the still-surviving trade guilds—the Maltsters and Weavers, Bonnetmakers and Wrights, for instance—whose members defended it at the Reformation.

On the south wall of the nave there is a memorial to the Stewarts of Minto. Frances Theresa Stewart caught the eye of Charles II, who paid her the compliment of taking her as the model for Britannia on the British coinage; but Charles did not impress her enough, and she married the Duke of Richmond instead.

In the lower church, the Blacader Aisle is believed to be on the site of

that burial ground of Cathures which St Ninian dedicated more than 1,500 years ago. St Kentigern's Tomb is covered by a beautifully embroidered silk cloth, with six embroidered kneeling-stools around it. Nearby, the St Kentigern Tapestry, like the tomb decorations, is modern work presented in the 1970s.

Another feature of the lower church is the present-day use made of its smaller side-chapels. The Chapel of St Andrew has been re-dedicated as a Nurses' Chapel, and its embroidered seat-covers show symbols of biblical medicinal herbs.

With all its ancient stone and woodwork, carvings and memorials, regimental colours associated with the city, and with the support it has received through the centuries from influential local organisations, Glasgow Cathedral is one of the most significant and historic buildings in Scotland; but it is also, as St Mungo intended his first little church at Glaschu—the 'Dear Green Place'—to be, somewhere people gather in humble and unflamboyant worship.

GLASGOW CROSS

More familiar to many people nowadays as the massed starting-point for the Glasgow Marathon, this crossroads at the foot of the High Street was once the heart of the city's mercantile area.

The only building which survives from the days—before the westward expansion of the city—when the council chambers, courthouse, prison and most fashionable coffee house were clustered round Glasgow Cross is the now-isolated Tolbooth Steeple of 1626. It stands a stately 126ft (38m) high and is topped by an ornamental crown tower. Until quite recently it was a great Glasgow tradition to join the carousing crowds at midnight on 31 December and hear the New Year 'rung in' on the steeple's carillon of bells.

Glasgow's mercat (or market) cross is a sturdy little octagonal tower, with balustraded roof and a heraldic unicorn on top of a central pillar, all designed as recently as 1929 by three members of the Glasgow Society of Lady Artists. The re-creation was long overdue, because the original mercat cross had been removed in 1659.

GLASGOW GREEN

Bounded on the south by the curving River Clyde, this oldest city park has facilities for rowing, bowling, hockey and football—Glasgow's two most famous football teams, Rangers and Celtic, both started here. Elsewhere, tree-lined avenues cross open grassy spaces. But Dassie Green on the east side is different. Its formal pathways run through lawns and flowerbeds.

The most notable buildings on the Green are the People's Palace (see page 48) and the former carpet factory, with walls of multicoloured brick, which was designed like the Doge's Palace in Venice.

The Green's memorials are many and varied. One stone shows where James Watt, on a morning stroll in 1765, suddenly thought of the improved steam-engine design which started the Industrial Revolution.

A long blue line along some paths and driveways represents the Peace Mile, to remind people of the International Year of Peace in 1986.

And when the last councillors of the old Glasgow Corporation stood down in 1975, 113 of them each planted a sugar maple to brighten the grassy banks of the Fleshers' Haugh.

GLASGOW SCHOOL OF ART

Renfrew Street
Architects and art historians from the world over visit this major building by Charles Rennie Mackintosh.

In 1896 a competition was announced for the design of a new School of Art on a spectacularly inconvenient site on the steep slope of one of Glasgow's drumlins—the glaciated hills on which so much of the city is built. Mackintosh had been a prize-winning evening-class pupil at the existing school; its principal, Francis Newbery, became a lifelong friend and admirer, and made sure that the governors accepted Mackintosh's design.

From the strong window treatment, imaginative skyline and functional yet at the same time decorative ironwork of the exterior, to the furniture, wood panelling and characteristic pendant lights inside the school, the whole place is, as a guided tour makes clear, the product of a single fertile mind—that of the undisputed leader of the Art Nouveau 'Glasgow Style'.

GLASGOW UNDERGROUND

The Glasgow 'Subway' had an ill-starred opening in December 1896. It ground to a halt after a derailment in the Inner Circle tunnel and a crash in the Outer!

The original cable-operated trains gave way to electricity in 1935, and the entire 15-station network was modernised in 1979.

A Subway Heritage Trail features above-ground walks from eight of the stations, including the delicious little red-sandstone Jacobean affair at St Enoch, retained after the modernisation.

Glasgow Green's Doulton Fountain, named after the china manufacturer who donated it to Glasgow for the 1888 International Exhibition in Kelvingrove Park. In 1891, a year after the terracotta structure was transferred to the Green, the figure of Queen Victoria which surmounted it was struck by lightning and the Doulton company paid for a hand-crafted replacement. Lifesize figures beneath the Queen represent the peoples of the British Empire

Children are given the run of the house, from the displays in the old-style kitchen, through various upper rooms with furniture and furnishings of generations gone by, including a Victorian nursery.

There are several fine booklets about the castle, including one on 16th- and 17th-century gardening; the garden itself, now in a suburban road rather than out in the country as it was when Haggs was built, is also used as an educational feature.

During weekends and holidays the museum's theme of learning-by-doing is extended to a series of workshops in an 18th-century cottage beside the castle. Here children busy themselves making butter and cheese, herb bags and rag dolls.

GLASGOW ZOO

Hamilton Road
Laid out on an attractive and lightly wooded hillside which dips down to the writhing course of the North Calder Water, Glasgow Zoo is on the extreme eastern edge of the city. The river is the boundary, and beyond it lies more open space, occupied by Calderbraes golf course.

The zoo is well through a long period of rebuilding and improvement; a fine new tiger house with pool and lounging platform overlooks the lower bend of the river, and there is a new enclosure for axis deer, for which pupils of a nearby school raised £1,850 in six weeks during 1986.

Supporters of the zoo also give financial assistance through the Animal Support Scheme. One, for instance, helps to keep Roger, the Vietnamese pot-bellied pig. A local tenants' association and a primary school support Kirsty, the Indian elephant. And there are certificates with the names of other supporters displayed throughout the zoo.

Out of doors, there are enclosures for lion, leopard, cheetah, rhino, camel, sheep, goat and several kinds of deer. Peacocks strut the lawns and their raucous screams suddenly ring through the trees.

Smaller wild cats and monkeys have indoor accommodation, and at the top of the hill the main focus of attention is the Tropical House. Here the zoo specialises in pythons and boas, and there is a window into the reptile breeding unit, with views of the very latest arrivals.

HAGGS CASTLE

St Andrew's Drive
If they keep fairly quiet, do not fidget and stay unobtrusively in the background, Haggs Castle is quite prepared to welcome adult visitors; but of all the museums in the city, this is the one given over almost completely to children.

Like so many now-public properties in Glasgow, the little mansion house once belonged to the Maxwells of Pollok. It was built—as its younger visitors are encouraged to find out from worksheets and quizzes—in the 1580s, and despite various rebuildings and extensions over the years much of the original masonry survives.

During the Second World War it was taken over by the Army; then it was converted into flats; and it was only in 1972 that Glasgow Corporation bought it for conversion into a museum.

In Haggs Castle, a museum designed especially for children, attractions include the rocking horse (top) in a Victorian nursery setting

HENRY WOOD HALL

Claremont Street
The tall spire reveals the original purpose of this building: it was opened in 1863 as the Trinity Congregational Church. After more than a century in that role, it was converted in 1978 into a base for the Scottish National Orchestra. The main part of the old church became a concert-hall, named after the famous conductor, whose portrait adorns one of the stairways.

The SNO rehearses in the building, but the concert-hall is also used for public performances by the BBC Scottish Symphony Orchestra as well as by smaller groups like the Scottish Early Music Consort and the Paragon Ensemble.

HIGH COURT

Saltmarket

With its massive Doric portico looking out over Glasgow Green, this is one of the city's buildings that now serves a different purpose from the one for which it was originally designed. For 30 years after its opening in 1814 it housed the City Chambers.

Jocelyn Square on its north side was originally Jail Square, because the main city prison used to be here too. Glasgow's public executions were held in the square, with sometimes tens of thousands of spectators trying to catch a glimpse of the scaffold handily built outside the prison door. The last of them was in 1865, when the city hangman disposed of the poisoner Dr Pritchard.

The present building, much altered in 1913, is open to the public when the High Court is in session.

HOGGANFIELD LOCH

Cumbernauld Road

This natural loch surrounded by parkland in the north-eastern suburbs is the source of the historic Molendinar Burn, which leaves it by an outflow pipe at the south-west corner and flows on its now so secretive way— largely underground— past the cathedral, through Glasgow Green and into the Clyde.

Made a public park in 1920, the loch and its grounds are a favourite family excursion place. Picnic parties often come to feed the swans, mallard, coots, geese and shrieking gulls which gather off the car park. The wooded island in the loch is a recognised bird sanctuary.

Facilities at Hogganfield include boating and coarse fishing for roach and pike. The fine 18-hole public golf course of Lethamhill stretches to the skyline, on the hillside where the springs which feed the loch rise. In the 19th century, Hogganfield was augmented by the waters of nearby Frankfield Loch, which was linked to it by an artificial channel; Frankfield is now just a 'wetland' site.

A wonderful recreation ground for people as well as ducks is provided by Hogganfield Loch — source of the Molendinar Burn — and its surrounding parkland

View from Glasgow Green of the imposing building with Doric portico designed by William Stark and serving from 1814 to 1844 as the City Chambers. It has since functioned as the High Court

HUTCHESONS' HALL

Ingram Street

One of the places to benefit most from the recent renovation of the city centre is Ingram Street, and this is the most significant building in it. The brothers George and Thomas Hutcheson were lavish 17th-century benefactors, best remembered for their endowment of famous boys' and girls' schools, which are now merged into one, and of the charitable institution known as Hutchesons' Hospital.

The impressive Ingram Street Hospital, replacing an earlier building elsewhere, was completed in 1805. It has recently been totally restored. There are now no residents, but the trustees still provide funds for something like 70 pensioners.

In 1983 the building passed into the ownership of the National Trust for Scotland. The ground floor now houses the NTS West of Scotland

headquarters, with an information centre and shop. The rebuilt hall is a venue for meetings, conferences and public concerts.

KELVIN HALL

Dumbarton Road

Once Glasgow's major exhibition hall, this substantial red-sandstone building is to reopen in the spring of 1988 as a massive indoor sports centre, complete with a 5,000-seat athletics arena.

It will also provide much-needed extra space for the city's Museum of Transport. Glasgow has the best collection anywhere in the world of Scottish-built cars like Albion, Argyll, Arrol-Johnston, Beardmore and Galloway. Its trams, buses, horse-drawn vehicles, steam locomotives and railway memorabilia can be shown to much better effect. A period street scene from 1938 and a historic display on the city's Subway system are also included.

A newly built mezzanine floor shows off the city's magnificent ship-model collection. Many of these— like the *Queen Mary* and the two *Queen Elizabeths*—were presentation pieces at the launch of their full-scale counterparts.

KELVINGROVE

Glasgow Corporation's great buying spree of public parks started in the 1850s when it took over land on the banks of the River Kelvin and engaged Sir Joseph Paxton, designer of the Crystal Palace in London, to lay out gardens, riverside and woodland walks.

Kelvingrove Park was added to and improved over the years, acquiring a bandstand, statues and memorials, and a pond shaped, curiously enough, like the island of Cyprus, which happened to be in the news at the time of the excavation.

The grounds were planted with elm, hornbeam, willow, mulberry, laurel and holly. London planes line Kelvin Way, and in April 1918 the 'suffrage oak' was planted near its junction with University Avenue to mark the granting of votes to women.

In 1888, 1901 and 1911 the park was the site of a series of International Exhibitions. Profits from the highly successful first two of these financed the replacement of a museum in Kelvingrove House with the massive Art Gallery and Museum which stands in the park today. In its first full year, the new building attracted no fewer than 1,113,688 visitors.

Its design was the subject of an open competition. Sadly, the opportunity was lost to have a building in the Art Nouveau 'Glasgow Style' which was then at its peak. What was accepted was a riotous red-sandstone affair whose roofline is ornamented to the point of positive eccentricity.

An often-repeated story about the scandal of the gallery's construction —of how the architect discovered only as the building was going up that he had drawn it back to front,

and committed suicide in the depths of career-ruined despair—has the minor drawback of being totally untrue.

The Art Gallery and Museum continues to be very popular, and it is a sign of the city's commitment to the arts that it can happily sustain both this and the Burrell.

The ground-floor Museum sections include natural history, archaeology, ethnography, a magnificent arms and armour collection, and a room devoted to the Glasgow Style which is a useful reminder that Charles Rennie Mackintosh was the leading but not by any means the only member of a movement which attracted many other artists and designers.

The tall central hall rises beyond the first floor, where gilded decorations on the stonework carry the names of famous composers and of the Incorporated Trades of the city—Tailors, Skinners, Gardeners, Barbers, Hammermen and the rest.

This first-floor level is the Art Gallery part of the building. Glasgow's stunning civic collection of paintings is displayed in a series of rooms devoted to Italian, Flemish, French, Dutch and British artists, including the Glasgow School and the Scottish Colourists. And all the Burrell Collection paintings, of course, are in their own gallery in Pollok Country Park!

But the single painting which attracts the greatest interest is Salvador Dali's *Christ of St John of the Cross*, an unusual view of the Crucifixion—seen from above—which is still almost as controversial as when it was bought for the city in the 1950s.

The Art Gallery and Museum (opposite) offers a huge and varied feast for mind and eye. Pursuits of a more relaxed nature may be enjoyed in Linn Park (above)

KING'S THEATRE

Bath Street
This is the principal theatre in the city, opened in 1904 and retaining, under the present ownership of the District Council, its beautifully maintained, elaborate Edwardian interior. Notables like Sarah Bernhardt, Harry Lauder, Jack Buchanan, Edith Evans, John Gielgud and Laurence Olivier have all appeared on its stage; and there is a full-scale winter pantomime season. The King's is made available for several weeks every spring and autumn to amateur societies which in most other cities would never have the chance of staging their productions in a major theatre: the Glasgow Grand Opera Society, for instance, and some that specialise in Gilbert and Sullivan, like the Savoy Club and the Orpheus Club, the latter of which, at various venues, has not missed an annual production since 1893.

LINN PARK

Clarkston Road and Old Castle Road
Like several of Glasgow's parks, this one was originally a private estate. Its 1820s mansion house is in use part of the time as a nature centre.

Linn Park is on a hillside site, with lawns and woodlands sweeping up from the winding valley of the White Cart Water. A public golf course occupies the highest ground; lower down there are attractive riverside and woodland pathways. Many of the park's activities are designed for its younger visitors, and there is an adventure playground for handicapped children.

Varied tree cover includes pine, chestnut, ash, rowan, beech, birch and cypress. The mixture of woodland and riverside attracts many birds, from woodpeckers to kingfishers, dippers to swallows.

At Court Hill on the northern edge of the park, a monument marks the place where, on 13 May 1568, Mary, Queen of Scots watched her army faring badly in the Battle of Langside.

MERCHANTS' HOUSE

West George Street
This is the name both of a fine Victorian building and of the mercantile guild which owns it. Around 1,200 members of the House have 40 charitable trusts and bursaries to administer.

When it was granted its 'letters of guildry' in 1605, the Merchants' House was in the Briggait. It still owns the only surviving part of that original building, the tall steeple with its high viewing gallery from which the merchants watched anxiously to see if their ships were on the incoming tide.

The splendid dark-wood hall on the first floor of the present building displays, in gilt lettering on varnished plaques, the names of 17th-century benefactors who left endowments to 'the poor of this Howse'.

Much of the building is let out as offices, and several of the rooms can be hired for meetings and conferences; but guided tours are usually available of a fascinating and historic building curiously unfamiliar to the citizens of Glasgow at large.

Mitchell Library displays a 15th-century printed book

MITCHELL LIBRARY

Kent Road
The burning-down of St Andrew's Halls in 1962 was a disaster for the concert-going public; but the destruction of the halls made possible the desperately needed expansion of the Mitchell Library which had previously occupied half the same city block.

Originally financed by one of Glasgow's Victorian tobacco barons, Stephen Mitchell, the library opened in its present completely modernised form in 1981. It is not only the headquarters of Glasgow District's 43-branch library network, but also the biggest public reference library in the whole of Europe, with a stock of over a million books.

The west side of the building, in Granville Street, was the former St Andrew's Halls. With its restored neo-Grecian façade, massive pillars and sculpture groups, this is now the entrance to the modern Mitchell Theatre.

things besides heavy engineering and Clydeside shipbuilding. The stories of the Tobacco Lords, who accumulated vast fortunes from Virginia and Carolina plantations before the American War of Independence, are told here. Products of the famous potteries, textile mills and magnificent foundries are all illustrated.

Behind the museum, the extravagant Winter Gardens had begun to deteriorate sadly by the start of the 1980s. The need to pump money into other projects like the Burrell gallery delayed the rescue work for a while; but in March 1987, after an expenditure of £715,650, the whole glorious conservatory was reopened to the public.

It is heated to allow palms, tree ferns, passionflowers, blue gum, umbrella plant and Norfolk Island pine to flourish, while the ground-level beds are bright with smaller flowers. The Winter Green Café has wrought-iron tables and chairs dotted around 'outside'. Being weather-free, the Winter Gardens are a popular place for a stroll, a snack meal or just a cup of coffee. Fashion shows, folk music and other lunchtime concerts are held from time to time; and it is even possible to arrange a wedding here.

Colourful and exotic plants make a glorious display in the Winter Gardens, opened in 1898 at the same time as the adjacent People's Palace. These were designed as a grand cultural centre for the working people of Glasgow. The People's Palace has the only collection of women's suffrage memorabilia in Scotland (upper right)

PEOPLE'S PALACE

Glasgow Green
Of all the museums in and around Glasgow, this one concentrates most closely, as its name implies, on the ordinary folk of the city.

A fine red-sandstone building, opened in 1898, it is backed by a splendid glass conservatory called the Winter Gardens, with soaring wrought-iron supports.

There is a strong political element in the museum's displays, especially from the time when Glasgow was in the forefront of demands for the extension of the franchise, the recognition of trade unions and the granting of votes for women. Historic banners and posters are on show, as well as copies of long-forgotten newspapers like *The Liberator*, *The Agitator* and *The Reformers' Gazette*.

The People's Palace is a treasure house of all kinds of items connected with the city, from a Roman bowl of AD150 found nearby on the Green, to mementoes of the Jacobite risings, football clubs and famous boxing matches, and one of Billy Connolly's stage costumes.

James Watt features strongly. As a young mathematical and scientific instrument-maker at the university, before his innovatory work on the steam-engine, he built the still-working pipe organ displayed in one of the ground-floor rooms.

The People's Palace is a fine reminder that in its heyday Glasgow made its money from many other

Sometimes seen keeping an eye on things is a Parks Department employee called Smudge. She is officially graded as a rodent operative; she is the only female member of the local branch of the General, Municipal, Boilermakers and Allied Trades Union; and also happens to be a cat.

Smudge's admirers among the Friends of the People's Palace commissioned a series of china replicas of her. A postcard photograph of the real cat surrounded by the life-size models is entitled 'Smudge and her chinas', a very neat pun in a city where 'china' is a slang word for friend.

Open to the public today as a museum, Provand's Lordship, just opposite the cathedral, exhibits domestic interiors and articles dating from 1500 to 1914; it also has a fine collection of period furniture

PROVAN HALL

Auchinlea Road
In the north-eastern fringes of Glasgow, the M8 motorway runs through a series of postwar housing schemes; but at one point there is a glimpse of a patch of woodland. These trees are in the grounds of Provan Hall, which is not only one of the oldest domestic properties in Scotland, but also a very close link with the city's ecclesiastical past.

In medieval times Glasgow Cathedral's 32 prebendaries or canons derived their incomes from church estates. The Prebend of Provan had the rents of no fewer than 2,000 acres. Provan Hall was his country residence, and this essentially pre-Reformation mansion house, where the north block has crow-stepped gables and a neat little round tower, and the courtyard is entered through a later gateway dated 1647, has remained almost miraculously preserved. This, despite all the massive changes that have taken place during the eastward extension of the city's built-up area.

Now owned by the National Trust for Scotland, Provan Hall is leased by Glasgow District Council as a community centre. The grounds have been re-landscaped, with a formal garden, ponds and a virtual maze of new pathways wandering through trees and flowering shrubs.

On a hill outside Queen's Park, the Langside Monument marks the site of the Battle of Langside. The lion on top of the monument faces Clincart Hill, where the forces of Mary, Queen of Scots gathered before the battle

PROVAND'S LORDSHIP

Castle Street
When his duties took him to the cathedral, the Prebend of Provan, whose country residence is described above, lived in what is now the oldest surviving house in the city centre.

Provand's Lordship (medieval spelling tended to be casual) was originally built in 1471 as the manse of an almshouse. After the Reformation it sank well down the social scale. In Victorian times it was used as an alehouse; in the early years of this century it was a sweet shop and fizzy-drinks factory; and a now-demolished lean-to once served as the home of the city hangman before degenerating into a junk shop.

Now, with its fabric carefully restored, Provand's Lordship is open as a museum. In its three floors of rooms there are furniture, paintings, prints and stained-glass panels from many eras in the city's history, as well as displays of the pottery and clay pipes which used to be manufactured nearby.

QUEEN'S PARK

Pollokshaws Road, Langside Avenue and Langside Drive
This was the first public park opened by Glasgow Corporation on the south side of the River Clyde and, like Kelvingrove, it was laid out to a landscape design by Sir Joseph Paxton.

It has woodlands, tree-lined avenues and grassy picnic areas on a sweeping hillside. The view from the flagpole on the uppermost terrace at 209 feet (64m) above sea level is wide-ranging.

The lady after whom the park is named was Mary, Queen of Scots, because it includes the site of the Battle of Langside, a sore defeat for her army. A district south of the park is still called Battlefield, and

just outside the park there is a tall monument to that engagement of 1568.

Camphill House, beside the boating pond, contains a fine collection of costumes; students have access to it and there are hopes of opening it fully as one of the city's museums.

ROBROYSTON

Despite its name, the district at the north-eastern tip of the city, where the built-up area gives way to rolling farmlands, has nothing to do with the outlaw Rob Roy MacGregor. A house here was the place where Sir William Wallace, who led the struggle against Edward I's army of occupation, was betrayed to the English forces in 1305.

In 1900, a tall Celtic cross, with a carving of the great two-handed sword always associated with him, was raised on the site of the house opposite Robroyston Mains. It was restored in 1986 with help from the Clan Wallace Society of the United States, where his name, as in Scotland, is still revered.

The Greek Grotto is one of several artificial ponds within the beautifully kept grounds of Rosshall Park, which also boasts heather gardens, woodland and nature trails

ROSSHALL PARK

Crookston Road
Completed in 1877 for the Cowan family, the red-sandstone mansion of Ross Hall is now a private hospital, with modern extensions. But it still looks down over the lavishly landscaped gardens laid out for the Cowans in the 1890s and extended by the shipbuilding Lobnitz family who took over ownership in 1908.

A virtually blank-cheque commission was given to the famous landscape gardening firm of Pullman and Sons, and their layout survives almost intact. A fine lawn, planted out with springtime bulbs, slopes down to a pond with wooded islands. All round there are flowering shrubs and specimen trees—copper beech, redwoods, cypress and maples—and one corner is laid out as a heather garden.

Pathways of sandstone slabs meander through the woodland fringe. And Pullmans created what look like natural outcrops of rock from synthetic sandstone; in a few places the outer skin has weathered away to show the artificial construction below.

One pathway, squeezing between rock walls and over tiny bridges, leads to the half-secret show-piece of the park, the secluded grotto specially built as the family's private swimming pool.

ROYAL HIGHLAND FUSILIERS MUSEUM

Sauchiehall Street
Behind what looks like a normal shop front there is a treasure house of military history in the museum of the regiment formed by the merger of the Royal Scots Fusiliers and the Highland Light Infantry.

Displays go back as far as Mar's Regiment of 1678, to which the Royal Scots Fusiliers trace their origin; and to the 73rd Highland Regiment (Macleod's Highlanders) formed in 1777, ancestor of the HLI.

The exhibition does not just concentrate on battle honours, although they are there in abundance, from the American War of Independence, through the Napoleonic campaigns, the siege of Gibraltar, India, the Crimea, South Africa and the major wars of the 20th century. Personalities are given their due, like Lt-Col Ainslie, commanding the 21st Royal North British Fusiliers at Inkerman, who reacted to a surprise Russian assault by grumbling to his officers, 'Damn

For bravery in Sudan, 1898, when he saved a wounded man, Captain Ruthven of 3rd HLI is honoured at the Royal Highland Fusiliers Museum

it, we must go in at these fellows first!' and fell mortally wounded in the thick of the battle.

Medals, uniforms, regimental silver, weaponry, plans and pictures of famous engagements—all add up to a lively and fascinating account of the regiments in which so many Glasgow men have served.

RUTHERGLEN

Although it is now within the boundaries of Glasgow District, Rutherglen has never been part of the city. It was a town of political and commercial significance when Glasgow concerned itself only with the affairs of the cathedral. In the Main Street, the replica market cross carries the date 1126, the year in which Ru'glen became a royal burgh.

A Heritage Trail visits the historic places in the town, like the parish church built on the site of a Norman-style predecessor where the Scottish Parliament deliberated in the year 1300.

Rutherglen Museum tells the story of the town and its organisations, and recalls a succession of long-gone industries such as coal mining, weaving, bleaching and printing, pottery, glass-making and chemicals.

Models recall the surprising fact that this town well up-river was once a flourishing centre of shipbuilding. Its northern boundary is the Clyde, and from the Clyde Walkway on the north bank, over a stretch of river well known to rowing clubs, there is a view across to the site of Seath's shipyard which, in the 46 years after 1856, launched no fewer than 327 vessels, from paddle-steamers and the royal yachts of Burma and Siam, to the *Lady of the Lake* and the *Raven*, which still operate the Ullswater services today.

SCOTLAND STREET SCHOOL

Scotland Street
Charles Rennie Mackintosh's striking design for this school opened in 1906 has fine leaded-window turrets, a sunny southern exposure for most of the classrooms, a neat little infants' entrance scaled down to suit its users, unexpected decorative work on the rear wall, and an archway on the east side with a bell tower which was his one miscalculation—the standard Glasgow School Board bell was too big to fit the space.

After the school closed in 1979 it was imaginatively converted into a museum of education. School parties come from as far away as Inverness come to period classrooms with Victorian, Edwardian, between-the-wars and Second World War furnishings and equipment. Pupils and teachers dress in appropriate costumes, and a normal class lesson of the time takes the children back to the schooldays of generations of their families long gone by.

Guided tours of the building, which retains most of its Mackintosh features, can be arranged if the school is contacted in advance.

SCOTTISH EXHIBITION AND CONFERENCE CENTRE

Finnieston Street
On the filled-in riverside site of the old Queen's Dock, this is the city's main exhibition area, with a large central hall and several smaller halls linked to it. There is an Exhibition Centre railway station, and the city-centre motorway is very close by.

The SECC has a remarkably varied programme, from trade fairs to medical conferences, from pop concerts to the Scottish National Orchestra Proms, and from sports events to the biennial Scottish Motor Show—very appropriate, since three Scottish makes (Albion, Kelvin and Halley) were first produced just across the street.

For 1988 only, the SECC is to be linked to the National Garden Festival site across the river by a pedestrian bridge.

602 (CITY OF GLASGOW) SQUADRON MUSEUM

Queen Elizabeth Avenue
602 was Glasgow's own squadron of the Royal Auxiliary Air Force, commemorated in a small museum at the rear of a present-day Air Training Corps squadron's base. Its volunteer pilots were involved in the very first air engagement over Britain during the Second World War, fought above the Firth of Forth in September 1939.

The museum has a wide range of photographs of the squadron's planes and personnel, from the Hawker days of the 1930s until the squadron was disbanded, during the jet age, in 1957.

There are medals, trophies, uniforms and some of the squadron's silver. Its rare distinction in the RAF of being allowed to wear the kilt—except on active service—is recalled. A Second World War pilot's 'escape kit' includes silk-scarf maps and a tiny compass built into a collar stud. Pride of place, perhaps, goes to one of the magnificent Rolls-Royce Merlin V12 engines—an appropriate display because the museum is actually within the area of a Rolls-Royce aero-engine factory.

SPRINGBURN MUSEUM

Ayr Street
Part of the local library, this museum traces the history of the one-time weaving village of Springburn through the days when

Below: Scottish Exhibition and Conference Centre. Right: Rolls-Royce Merlin V12 engine in the museum for 602 (City of Glasgow) Squadron

it was Europe's greatest railway-locomotive building centre. Workshops such as Cowlairs, North British Locomotive and Hyde Park exported something like 18,000 locomotives to railway companies all over the world. Completed locomotives were taken by road to Finnieston Street, and loaded onto ships by the massive hammer-head crane that still stands near the Scottish Exhibition and Conference Centre.

Tragically, as steam faded from the scene and diesels and diesel-electrics took its place, Springburn reacted far too late to the inevitable trend. Not a single locomotive comes out of Springburn today, and even the last of its railway repair shops has gone.

School life from Victorian times to the Second World War is displayed at the Museum of Education, housed in the Scotland Street School designed by Mackintosh

STIRLING'S LIBRARY

Queen Street and Royal Exchange Square
This is Glasgow's biggest public lending library, based on a collection bequeathed to the city in 1791 by the merchant Walter Stirling and housed in one of its finest buildings. At its heart is the 1780 mansion of William Cunninghame, who made a huge fortune at the time of the American War of Independence by buying up all the stocks of Virginia tobacco held by the city's nervous merchants, and reselling it later at a 700 per cent profit.

In 1817 the house became the Glasgow headquarters of the Royal Bank of Scotland. And in 1829 it was greatly extended as the city's Royal Exchange, where most of the business in iron, steel, coal and sugar was carried out. Royal Exchange Square was laid out in dignified style around it.

The old Cunninghame mansion now has a massive pillared entrance in front of it, and the library lending hall behind. This was originally the main hall of the Royal Exchange, and retains the finest ornamental barrel-vaulted ceiling in the city.

STOCK EXCHANGE

Nelson Mandela Place (formerly St George's Place)
One of the most exuberant buildings in the city centre, this Venetian Gothic extravaganza with its series of pointed-arch arcades was completed over a 30-year period from 1876.

Most of the interior space is now taken up by other modern offices. The Stock Exchange itself is on the first floor of the building's Edwardian western extension. It is the only 'trading floor' in Scotland and one of only three in Britain, part of the International Stock Exchange

formed by an amalgamation in 1973.

Dealings these days are done on computer screens, but there is a small viewing gallery and visitors are welcome during normal trading hours.

STRATHCLYDE UNIVERSITY

George Street, Montrose Street and Richmond Street
Although it achieved university status as recently as 1964, this institution was founded in 1796, in accordance with the will of Professor John Anderson—'Jolly Jack Phosphorus' to the students in his physics classes—who had been on the staff of Glasgow University and heartily disliked most of his teaching colleagues and the over-academic way the university was run.

Anderson was a pioneer in

Opposite: floodlighting reveals Stirling's Library, with its grand portico added when William Cunninghame's mansion became the Royal Exchange. Inset: the library's splendid coffered ceiling

technical and evening-class education, and Strathclyde is a science-and-technology-based university today.

But it also takes a keen interest in the arts. Among the cluster of buildings it occupies, right in the city centre, is the Collins Gallery, housing many public exhibitions of paintings, prints, sculpture and photographs. The university also runs a very varied programme of concerts, lectures, poetry readings and films.

THE TENEMENT HOUSE

Buccleuch Street
The National Trust for Scotland's properties open to the public vary from castles and landscaped gardens to country estates and mountain ranges. But this one is simply a city-centre flat, lived in from 1911 to 1965 by Miss Agnes Toward.

It is in the district of Garnethill—named, oddly enough, after Thomas Garnet, the first professor of natural philosophy at Anderson's College (see above). In 1810 he was commemorated in the building of an observatory here that has now disappeared.

Miss Toward's house is in a red-sandstone building completed in 1892. Typical of turn-of-the-century design, it has a hall, parlour, bedroom, kitchen and bathroom, all furnished as they might have been (and in most details actually *were*) during her lifetime, with gas lighting, a cast-iron kitchen range, oak and mahogany woodwork, lace curtains, a rosewood piano—and the masses of letters, newspaper cuttings, bills, recipes and schoolbooks she could never bring herself to throw away.

THEATRE ROYAL

Hope Street
This is the oldest surviving theatre name in Glasgow. The first Theatre Royal in Dunlop Street went through a bizarre period when there was one auditorium at ground level, and a rival company putting on different performances at the same time on a stage in the basement. In a long-standing tradition of Glasgow

theatre, that building was engulfed by fire. A second Theatre Royal elsewhere went the same way. And the present building, on a third site, has been burned out three times since it was first put up in 1867.

After being taken over in the 1950s as the original base of Scottish Television, it was completely restored in 1975 to become the headquarters of Scottish Opera, with a fine new staircase and elegant foyer added to its renovated Victorian auditorium. It is also used for performances by another national company based in Glasgow, Scottish Ballet.

THIRD EYE CENTRE

Sauchiehall Street
Founded in 1975, and occupying part of the once highly regarded Grecian Building designed by Alexander 'Greek' Thomson about 110 years previously, this was Glasgow's first contemporary arts centre.

It has two exhibition galleries, a studio-style theatre, a wholefood cafeteria and a small but well-stocked bookshop concentrating on the arts, politics and Scottish subjects of almost every kind.

Many of the Third Eye's exhibitions of painting, sculpture and photography go on to tour Scotland and are accompanied by specially published books.

The centre is closely associated with Mayfest, Glasgow's three-week international festival in May, less grand than its Edinburgh counterpart, but lively with dance and drama, music and literary events all over the city.

TRADES HOUSE

Glassford Street
Home of its craftsmen's guilds, the Trades House of Glasgow is the only major building by Robert Adam to survive in the city. Although his 1794 interiors have been partly remodelled, the façade is virtually unchanged.

Originally, there were 15 Incorporated Trades in Glasgow, but the Mariners faded out soon after the House was officially recognised in 1605. In modern times, the 14 remaining Trades are almost entirely charitable organisations, each with its own pensioners.

The coats of arms of the 14 Trades form a major element in the decoration of the house. They appear on a fine stained-glass window facing the double staircase; on the dome of the elegant banqueting hall which also has a silk frieze showing the various craftsmen at work; and on the intricately carved benches in the entrance hall, made by Belgian woodworkers who were refugees in Glasgow during the First World War.

The main rooms are often used for functions; although visitors are welcome to have a guided tour, the availability should be checked in advance.

TRONGATE

Although it is a much older thoroughfare, this short street took its present name because it was on the way to the tron, or weigh-bar, installed at Glasgow Cross in 1491. Part of it later became known as the Plainstanes, which the wealthy Tobacco Lords—looked down upon by the old aristocracy of the city as being 'in trade'—took as their personal preserve, sweeping aside any lesser mortals who impeded their scarlet-cloaked progress.

Curiously placed astride the pavement, the Tron Steeple is all that remains of a church burned down in 1793 when a prank by the young bloods of the local Hell-Fire Club got spectacularly out of hand. A new church was built a little way back from the street, and it has now been converted into the Tron Theatre.

Articles on display in Tenement House include this rosewood piano and the cup and saucer. All of the present contents could have belonged (and many did belong) to Miss Toward, who lived in the flat from 1911 for over 50 years

UNIVERSITY OF GLASGOW

University Avenue
Founded in 1451, this is the second-oldest university in Scotland, that of St Andrews having been established 40 years before. In its earliest days, classes were held in the chapter-house of Glasgow Cathedral. Then there was a brief foray to Rottenrow—curiously enough, in the heart of the city-centre district where Strathclyde University now stands. From 1470 onwards the university was in the High Street, but in 1863 the then-decaying buildings were sold off to be the site of a railway goods yard!

With part of the proceeds, the university authorities bought the present site on Gilmorehill, overlooking Kelvingrove Park. As was to happen a generation later with the Art Gallery and Museum across the wooded valley of the Kelvin, local architects were highly disgruntled that the commission to design the new building should have gone to a London practice: Sir George Gilbert Scott started the Gothic Revival design and his son, John Oldrid Scott, continued it.

The university complex was added to right into the 1970s, and one of the most notable buildings is the Hunterian Art Gallery. Its collection of paintings is based on the ones presented in the 18th century by Dr William Hunter, but now includes a fine selection of 19th- and 20th-century French and Scottish works.

The print collection is the most substantial in Scotland, with more than 15,000 items, many of them by James McNeill Whistler.

Most important of all, the gallery's tower includes a splendid re-creation of the nearby house once occupied by Charles Rennie Mackintosh—even to his original windows and front door, which is at first sight puzzlingly located, well above road-level and with no means of access short of levitation.

The university has gone to great lengths to furnish the rooms with mostly original but occasionally replica tables, chairs, cupboards, cabinets, light fixtures and decorations in cool Art Nouveau colour schemes both by Mackintosh and by his wife Margaret, an accomplished designer herself.

Across the road in the Victorian part of the university, the Hunterian

A magnificent westerly view of the Glasgow University skyline is dominated by the tower designed by Gilbert Scott, completed by his son Oldrid. Right: the Room de Luxe of the Willow Tearooms offers afternoon tea with the Edwardian elegance of Miss Cranston's day

Museum shows how William Hunter's interests extended well beyond the field of art. The exhibits have been greatly added to over the years, but the astonishing Coin Gallery, with its 30,000 coins and medals going back to the time of Ancient Greece, is almost entirely Hunter's own.

Other displays include items brought back from the Pacific by Captain Cook, the story of the Forth-to-Clyde construction of the Romans' Antonine Wall, and the 325-million-year-old fossilised shark found recently in the town of Bearsden on the city's northern edge.

Public concerts and exhibitions of many kinds are also held in the university, which has a long tradition of public access: it opened William Hunter's collection in 1807 as the first museum of any kind in the city.

million years old. It was decided to protect and display them rather than simply cover them up again, and the building called the Fossil Grove still stands at the west end of the park. Beside it, the old quarry has been planted out as a colourful rock- and water-garden.

Elsewhere, Victoria Park has sports grounds and a neatly laid-out boating and model-yacht pond with islands and rustic bridges. There are tree-lined walks and an arboretum, formal flowerbeds and an example of that familiar Scottish landscape feature, an artificial hill placed to provide a pleasant view.

PS WAVERLEY

Lancefield Quay
The Belfast steamers used to sail from Lancefield Quay in the heart of the city. Now it is the base of two splendidly nostalgic cruising ships.

Operated by the same company, the *Balmoral* was launched in 1949 and is modelled on the design of a lavish private yacht. Most of her sailings are in the south—from Llandudno and Caernarfon, for instance—but she has a programme of Clyde cruises in September. Both ships tie up for the winter at Lancefield Quay.

This formal garden with its brightly coloured flowers seems a world away from the roots and stumps of extinct trees in the Fossil Grove, yet both are to be found in Victoria Park.

WILLOW TEAROOMS

Sauchiehall Street
At the turn of the century, Glasgow's tea rooms were much grander and much more extensive in what they offered their clientele than the name suggests. Lunch and dinner rooms, smoking and billiard rooms were often provided as well.

Undoubtedly the finest was this Art Nouveau gem which Charles Rennie Mackintosh designed for Miss Kate Cranston, the dominating figure in the business. Its name was a reminder that the original 'saughs' of Sauchiehall were willows; but Mackintosh—and his wife—also took Rossetti's haunting sonnet about the willow wood as the theme for the decoration of the show-piece Room de Luxe.

Over the years, all the 'Miss Cranston's' closed down; but the Willow has been rescued. The original Mackintosh façade has been restored, and although the ground floor is now occupied by a jeweller's shop, the Room de Luxe is a tea room once again. Among the replica Mackintosh furniture, it is easy to drift back to the Edwardian era, when Glasgow's finest architect put his talent at the disposal of the city's most enterprising caterer.

VICTORIA PARK

Victoria Park Drive North and Westland Drive
This is one of the parks which Glasgow did not plan for itself, but acquired during its relentless gathering-in of what had previously been small, independent burghs beyond its historic boundaries.

Partick Burgh took over the land from a privately owned estate in 1886. As was also done in the city, labouring work was offered to unemployed shipyard men. The park opened to the public in 1887, the year of Queen Victoria's Golden Jubilee.

When a pathway was being dug across a disused quarry, some curious stone-like tree stumps were revealed. They turned out to be fossil remains something like 330

The 693-ton *Waverley* is the last sea-going paddle-steamer in the world. She was launched in 1946, sailed the Clyde until the end of 1973, and was then sold off to a group of steamer enthusiasts for precisely £1.

Their original idea was to use her as a floating museum-cum-restaurant, but the Waverley Steam Navigation Company was soon formed and the ship was refitted for a regular cruising schedule. Now she alternates between spells of cruising from Glasgow to places like Helensburgh, Dunoon, Rothesay, Tighnabruaich, Millport, Brodick and Ayr—traditional 'doon the watter' destinations for generations of city holidaymakers—and similar scheduled sailings along the south coast of England, the Bristol Channel and the Thames.

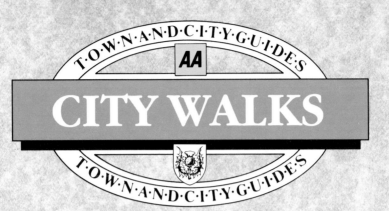

CITY WALKS

*Nature and civilisation combine to produce a wonderfully
rich feast in peaceful Pollok Country Park, just three
miles from the heart of Glasgow*

Church and Commerce

T̲his walk starts and finishes in the very heart of the city, and takes in Glasgow's cathedral, its oldest house, its principal newspaper, its centre of administration, and many other points of interest. There is much to see. As with all these walks, do take great care when crossing roads—use lights or pedestrian crossings whenever possible and always check the traffic flow. Many streets in the city are one-way.

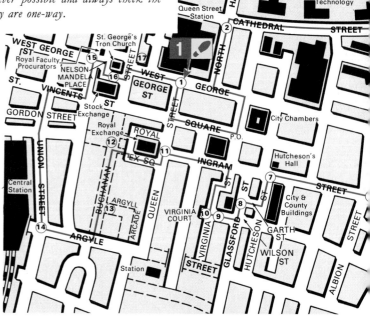

*2¼ miles/4km
Allow 2 hours*

Start at the north-west corner of George Square, outside Queen Street Station, and walk round the square in an anti-clockwise direction.

1 GEORGE SQUARE
The square is full of impressive statues. You pass Robert Peel, Queen Victoria and her consort Prince Albert, James Watt, Robert Burns, Field Marshal Lord Clyde, Gladstone and others less well remembered today. Note the inscription on the statue of the now-forgotten MP, James Oswald— 'erected by a few friends 1855'. The Victorians were very fond of that sort of gesture.

On the east side of the square is the City Chambers (William Young, 1883–8), the administrative centre of the city of Glasgow and the office of its principal citizen, the Lord Provost. Guided tours are available.

Leave George Square by North Hanover Street and at the first junction turn right into Cathedral Street. Walk to the end of this street, keeping right where the road divides.

2 CATHEDRAL STREET
This is a very educational thoroughfare. On the right are the campus buildings of the University of Strathclyde—truly a university within a city—and on the left the Central College of Commerce, the Glasgow College of Food Technology, and Allan Glen's School.

At the T-junction cross the road and enter the cathedral precinct. (The cathedral is just off the map.)

3 CATHEDRAL PRECINCT
To the left as you enter the precinct is the massive structure of the Royal Infirmary, designed by James Miller and begun in 1907. Ahead is Glasgow Cathedral, the only pre-Reformation church in the city. Its foundation dates back to 543 when St Mungo established a religious order here. The cathedral is open throughout the year and admission is free.

In Cathedral Square are more statues, including one to the explorer David Livingstone, who was born in Scotland. Here also is

the entrance to the Necropolis, or burial ground. It contains many vast and impressive tombs and monuments and is well worth exploring.

Recross the road to visit Provand's Lordship directly opposite.

4 PROVAND'S LORDSHIP
This is the oldest existing house in Glasgow. It was built in 1471 by Bishop Andrew Muirhead, and it is believed that Mary Queen of Scots lived here for a while in 1566. The house is open every day, and admission is free.

On leaving Provand's Lordship, turn right and walk down Castle Street.

5 CASTLE STREET
Across the road is an equestrian statue of King William III—the oldest of its kind in the city. It was erected in about 1735 and was moved to this site from the Trongate later.

At the junction go straight ahead into High Street; at the next junction turn right into Ingram Street.

6 INGRAM STREET
This street is named after an 18th-century Lord Provost. Looking up the second street on the right, Albion Street, you will see the offices and print works where the *Glasgow Herald* and *Evening Times* newspapers are produced six days a week. The *Herald* recently celebrated its bicentenary.

The great tower of the City Chambers, built in Italian Renaissance style

No.137 Ingram Street is a listed building dating from 1855. It has recently been sandblasted and now looks really splendid. Opposite Hutcheson Street is Hutcheson's Hall, now the West of Scotland offices of the National Trust for Scotland. The building dates from 1802. The statues are of the two Hutcheson brothers, who established a hospice here in the mid-17th century.

Turn left into Hutcheson Street.

7 HUTCHESON STREET
On your left are the City and County Buildings—a typically massive Victorian edifice, built originally (in 1842) to house civil servants. The

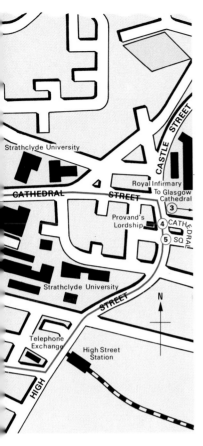

frontage on Hutcheson Street has no fewer than 29 bays, with the middle 9 having large Corinthian columns.
Turn right into Garth Street.

8 TRADES HOUSE
Facing you as you walk down the short Garth Street is Trades House, whose Adam façade, dating from 1791, is almost intact.
Turn left into Glassford Street, right into Wilson Street and cross Virginia Street.

9 VIRGINIA STREET
As you enter Virginia Street from Wilson Street you face Nos.31–53, which date from about 1820 and are the best surviving example of that period in the city centre.
Cross Virginia Street to enter Virginia Court.

10 VIRGINIA COURT
This small court has a distinctly 19th-century feel about it, with its cobblestones, ironwork and the still-visible grooves made by cartwheels.
Return to Virginia Street, turn left and walk up to Ingram Street. Turn left again and walk to the junction with Queen Street. Cross into Royal Exchange Square.

11 ROYAL EXCHANGE SQUARE
The building facing you as you walk along Ingram Street is the former Royal Exchange, dating from 1827 but containing within its eastern part a town villa of 1775. The exchange was a meeting place for businessmen and traders, but the building underwent a

transformation in the 1950s to become Stirling's Library. The statue in front of the building is of the Duke of Wellington.

Royal Exchange Square was built in 1830; the north and south sides are almost identical rows of houses over shops, gracefully proportioned and very pleasing in their symmetry.
Leave the square by one of the two archways into Buchanan Street, and turn left down the pedestrian precinct.

12 BUCHANAN STREET
The large Royal Bank building closing the west end of Royal Exchange Square was built in 1827, at which time the bank moved here from the Royal Exchange building behind it.

Buchanan Street is a smart shopping centre. At No.91 the Clydesdale Bank occupies a fine sandstone building originally designed as one of the celebrated Cranston's tea rooms in 1896.
Turn left into Argyll Arcade.

13 ARGYLL ARCADE
The arcade is entered through an aluminium canopy. It was built by John Baird in 1827 and features a fine glazed hammerbeam roof with splendid cast-ironwork. The arcade is a very pleasant shopping area, with numerous jewellers.
Return to Buchanan Street and at its foot turn right into Argyle Street. Take the second right into Union Street.

The Buchanan Street area has some very tempting shops in it

14 UNION STREET
Ahead of you as you turn into Union Street is the bridge carrying the rail lines out of Central Station. Familiarly known as the 'Hielan'man's Umbrella', it was formerly used as a meeting place for Highlanders who had moved to Glasgow to live and work.

At Nos.84–100 Union Street are the 'Egyptian Halls', designed by Alexander 'Greek' Thomson and built in 1871. An Egyptian building from a Greek-influenced architect may sound anomalous but the name merely indicates the classical influence dominating the design.

At the corner of Union Street and Gordon Street is, at present, the sad sight of what should be one of the glories of this walk, the Ca d'Oro

building. The name means House of Gold, and gilt was extensively used in the decoration of this John Honeyman design dating from 1872, with its fine, almost cathedral-like windows another splendid feature. The building was seriously damaged by fire in March 1987 but it is hoped that full restoration will be possible.
Cross the always busy Gordon Street and at the next junction turn right into St Vincent Street, then left into West Nile Street and right again into West George Street.

15 ROYAL FACULTY OF PROCURATORS
Situated on the corner of West George Street and West Nile Street, this building, dating from 1854, has a detailed exterior design which owes much to the Venetian influence.
Cross West Nile Street and enter Nelson Mandela Place.

16 NELSON MANDELA PLACE
Formerly St George's Place, this square was renamed in 1986 after the black African freedom fighter—a move which caused considerable controversy at the time. On its south side is the Glasgow Stock Exchange, a striking example of Victorian Gothic design with its arcade of pointed arches on the ground level and smaller arches on the upper floors. The interior of the building has been entirely rebuilt and refurbished while leaving the magnificent exterior intact—a sensitive piece of work.

The square is principally occupied by St George's Tron Church (presumably not to be renamed!), an 1807 design by William Stark which owes more than a little to Wren. A board outside the church proclaims it as 'a place of peace in the city of noise'.
Cross Buchanan Street and continue along West George Street to the end of the walk in George Square.

17 WEST GEORGE STREET
If you look north up Buchanan Street it may appear to be unfinished in aspect; indeed it is. There are plans for a major redevelopment here including a full-scale concert hall, which it is hoped might be completed in time for the celebrations of Glasgow's 'European City of Culture' year in 1990.

On the south side of West George Street is a new Clydesdale Bank building, a good example of modern commercial architecture with much use of pink granite and bronze-tinted glass. On the corner with George Square is the Merchants' House, home of Glasgow Chamber of Commerce. It is topped by a golden sailing ship, a reminder of the importance to Glasgow of its waterways.
The walk ends where it started in George Square.

Going West

*T*his walk travels westward out of the city centre into the area
developed in the 19th century as Glasgow expanded. It passes the largest
office building in Glasgow, the largest public library in Europe, and a
perfectly preserved Victorian tenement flat. There is much variety on this
walk but, being Glasgow, there are some rather steep slopes includ d—be
warned!

2¼ miles/4km
Allow 2 hours

*The walk starts at the main entrance to
the Central Hotel in Hope Street.*

1 CENTRAL STATION
This complex, including the hotel,
was built just over 100 years ago for
the Caledonian Railway to link
Glasgow with the south. It is a
splendid example of Victorian
railway architecture—grand and
imposing.
   *Walk north up Hope Street and turn
left into St Vincent Street.*

2 ST VINCENT STREET (EAST)
Turning into St Vincent Street you
see immediately opposite at
Nos.142–4 the extraordinary
building known as the Hatrack. It is
ten storeys high but only three bays
wide; the design incorporates the
minimum of stonework so as to let
as much light in as possible. Next
door, in contrast, is the Scottish
Amicable building, a recent
development with many tinted glass
panels. Its designer made the bay
next to the Hatrack the same width
as the older building to help them
harmonise as far as possible. This is
a remarkable blend of old and new.
   *Climb St Vincent Street as far as
Blythswood Street, then turn right up to
the top of the hill and Blythswood Square.
Walk round the square in an
anticlockwise direction.*

3 BLYTHSWOOD SQUARE
The square dates from 1823 to 1829
and was designed by John Brash.
Everything seems well
proportioned, perhaps notably the
fine east side which is wholly
occupied by the Royal Scottish
Automobile Club. This is the
nearest square to the city centre to
feature much in the way of
greenery—a pleasure to the eye
indeed.
   *Leave Blythswood Square by Douglas
Street and turn right to rejoin St Vincent
Street.*

4 ST VINCENT STREET (WEST)
On either side of Douglas Street are
imposing buildings dominating this
end of St Vincent Street. To the left
(east) is the massive church designed
by 'Greek' Thomson and built in
1858. The church with its many
pillars sits high atop a meeting hall.
The tower is a weird
conglomeration of pinnacles,
colonnades and mini-spires topped
off with an odd elongated dome. It
shouldn't work but somehow it
does. Facing the church is the new
Britoil headquarters building,
opened in autumn 1986 and the
largest block in Glasgow. It is not so
high as to overpower the church
utterly, and the exterior is relieved
with several balcony gardens.
   *Continue down St Vincent Street,
cross the M8 motorway and turn right
into North Street.*

5 NORTH STREET
This section of the M8 is one of the
busiest stretches of urban motorway
in Britain. It provides Glasgow with
exceptionally good communications
to other parts of Scotland and to the
south. As you walk up North Street
you pass a line of birch trees
struggling hard to survive in the city
environment.
   *Turn left into Kent Road to walk
round the Mitchell Library, turning right
into Granville Street.*

6 THE MITCHELL LIBRARY
The Mitchell is the largest public
reference library in Europe. Its
founder, Stephen Mitchell, who

*The copper-domed Mitchell Library, an
imposing building inside and out, houses
over a million volumes*

died in 1874, is commemorated by a
bust in the entrance hall. The
library's dome is surmounted by the
figure of Minerva, Goddess of
Wisdom. The western section of the
library, which now contains a
theatre, café and meeting rooms,
was formerly the St Andrew's Halls
and was rebuilt after a fire some
years ago. The handsome façade
fortunately survived; on it are
inscribed names connected with the
arts, including Michelangelo,
Raphael, Mozart, Bach and
Beethoven.
   Turn right into Berkeley Street.

7 66 BERKELEY STREET
This house was the scene of a
murder in 1865. The perpetrator, Dr
Pritchard, was hanged for his crime.
   *Rejoin North Street; there turn left.
Pass under the 'bridge to nowhere'.*

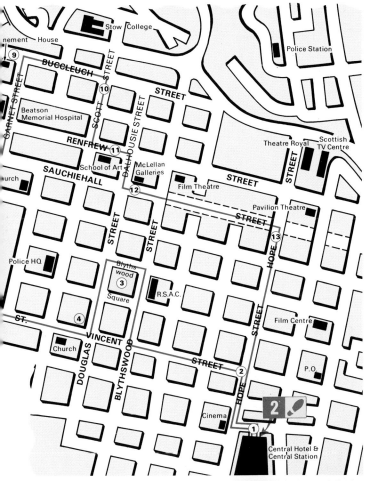

Charles Rennie Mackintosh. He won a competition to design the building—at the age of 28—and did the entire interior as well as the building itself. Mackintosh drawings and furniture are on display inside. The school had to be completed in two phases due to difficulty with funding. The east wing opened in 1899 and the west wing, with the attic storey, opened in 1907–9.

Turn left from Dalhousie Street into Sauchiehall Street and walk through the pedestrian precinct to Hope Street.

12 SAUCHIEHALL STREET

Sauchiehall Street is one of Glasgow's premier shopping centres. The name is believed to come from two Scots words meaning 'a willow meadow'. There is little resemblance to a meadow today but at least the pedestrianisation of the street makes it possible to wander along it in comparative peace.

The large building on the left as you enter Sauchiehall Street, like the Ca d'Oro in Walk 1, unfortunately seriously damaged by fire, contains the McLellan Galleries, with a bust of Queen Victoria above the door. Restoration is under way and it is hoped that this very popular venue, much used for concerts and lectures, will be brought back into full use before long.

Across the road at No.217 are the Willow Tearooms, another C R Mackintosh design. The ground floor is today a jeweller's shop but the tea rooms on the first floor are still serving refreshment to thirsty shoppers. The building was designed by Mackintosh in 1903 as the 'flagship' of the Cranston tea-room business, run by Miss Kate Cranston and a great feature of Glasgow life in the early years of this century.

There are often musicians busking in Sauchiehall Street, ranging from classical violinists through folk singers to brass players, and quite often you will find a pavement chalk artist at work— work always destined to be ephemeral.

Turn right into Hope Street and walk back down to the Central Hotel and the end of the walk.

13 HOPE STREET

Hope Street is a main northbound artery for traffic and always seems to be busy whatever the time of day. Central Station and its hotel draw the eye as you walk down, but first look across the street to Nos.170–2. This fine building—an example of the early use of reinforced concrete— dates from 1905 and was designed by James Salmon and Galt Gillespie. The walls and floors are just four inches thick.

The walk ends outside the Central Hotel. Refreshments are served here throughout the day and the interior is spacious.

8 GLASGOW'S LEANING TOWER

There are plans to develop the rather sad-looking 'bridge to nowhere' with two storeys of offices linked to a larger block in Newton Street. Before you turn right to recross the M8, cross to the north side of Sauchiehall Street for a look at Glasgow's own leaning tower— albeit a very small one. This drinking fountain with four clock faces was erected 'in honour of Sir Charles Cameron Bart in recognition of his many services to this city and to Scotland'.

At the lights turn right to recross the M8 into Sauchiehall Street. Turn left from Sauchiehall Street into Garnet Street (NTS sign on the corner) and walk up the very steep brae, over two crossroads, and down an equally steep brae to turn left in Buccleuch Street to the Tenement House.

9 THE TENEMENT HOUSE

See the Gazetteer, pages 52–3, for details of the Tenement House, an amazingly well-preserved example of Victorian life. The building containing it was built in 1892 and is typical of the period.

Walk back along Buccleuch Street, passing the imposing façade of the former Garnethill School—a real 'abandon hope all ye who enter here' building!—and take the second right into Scott Street. Another climb and descent is needed, but the views southwards over the city are very extensive on a good day.

Sauchiehall Street pavement artist at work on feline ephemera

10 'GARNET HILL' MURAL

On your right in Scott Street, just past the present entrance to Garnethill School, is a rather fine mural on a house-end. It is geologically based with the names of many precious and semiprecious stone and the words 'Garnet Hill' in the centre.

Turn left into Renfrew Street and right into Dalhousie Street to walk back down to Sauchiehall Street.

11 GLASGOW SCHOOL OF ART

In Renfrew Street is the Glasgow School of Art, perhaps the finest example we have of the work of

Glasgow Green and the Clyde

This walk encounters Glasgow's river, its oldest public open space, its own local history museum, a building which would look more at home in Venice, and the very heart of the old city.

2 miles/3km
Allow 1½ hours

The walk starts in St Enoch Square, just off Argyle Street. Walk south across the square and leave it by Dixon Street to walk down to the River Clyde.

1 ST ENOCH SQUARE

It is believed that St Enoch Square was named after St Thenew, the mother of St Mungo (see Walk 1). The main terminus of the Glasgow and South Western Railway was formerly here; it closed in 1966. After that the square languished somewhat, but it is now being revived with the building of a major shopping centre and an ice rink. The former subway station, a rather jolly little building, has been conserved and is in busy use as a travel centre.

At the foot of Dixon Street, cross Clyde Street and turn left by the river along the walkway.

2 CUSTOM HOUSE QUAY

This part of the riverbank is known as Custom House Quay after its former purpose. The walkway is constructed of cobbles which are picturesque rather than comfortable on the feet.

The fascinating history of the Customs and Excise here takes in the names of the poet Robert Burns—an exciseman by trade— and of his contemporary, Alexander Findlater, the subject of Burns's poem 'The De'il's Awa' wi' the Exciseman'.

Before the quay was closed in the 1960s, it was used by small steam 'puffers' carrying stone chips for building and road construction. It is hard to imagine today that 250 years ago there was a stream, the St Enoch Burn, running down to the river here past an open area known as Ropework Green. The land was owned by James Oswald, whose statue in George Square, 'erected by a few friends', we met at the start of Walk 1.

After passing the Jamaica footbridge you rejoin the roadway by the *Carrick*, a fine sailing ship built in the 1860s and now permanently moored here as the headquarters of the Royal Naval Volunteer Reserve (RNVR) Club. Across the river you can see the golden dome of Glasgow's new mosque—a touch of the Orient in the west of Scotland.

At the next road bridge over the river (Victoria Bridge), recross Clyde Street to have a look at the Briggait Shopping Centre.

3 BRIGGAIT SHOPPING CENTRE

This was opened by HRH Princess Margaret in June 1986. It contains about 50 shops, cafés, etc, and is well worth a visit. It is closed all day Tuesday but is open the other six days of the week.

Continue along Clyde Street to the Albert Bridge and cross Saltmarket to enter Glasgow Green.

4 CLYDE STREET

The street was once the site of a horse fair, with animals regularly bought and sold here. On the corner with Saltmarket is the High Court. In the 19th century there was a gallows outside the court; the last criminal to be hanged in public here, in 1865, was the infamous Dr Pritchard, who poisoned his wife and mother-in-law.

Walk up the main avenue of Glasgow Green to the tall Nelson Monument.

5 NELSON'S COLUMN ON THE GREEN

Glasgow Green is the oldest public open space in the city and one of the oldest in Europe. Its long and fascinating history is told in a leaflet obtainable at the People's Palace (see below). Pass the Doulton Fountain, erected for the Great Exhibition of 1888 but now sadly only a derelict shadow of its former glory. Queen Victoria, atop the fountain, has been 'decorated' with a lightning conductor.

Nelson's Column on the Green was erected in 1807—the first of its kind in Britain, predating the much more famous column in London's Trafalgar Square. On its four sides are carved in huge letters the names of Nelson's victories—Aboukir, Copenhagen, St Vincent and Trafalgar. Near the column is a large boulder commemorating the invention of the steam condenser by James Watt in 1765.

Past Nelson's Column, take the right-hand path following the line of the river. Pass the St Andrew's Suspension Bridge on the right and the offices of the Glasgow Humane Society on the left. Then take the second path on the left to cross the Green.

6 THE RIVERSIDE

This part of the Clyde is regularly used by rowing clubs, and on summer evenings or at weekends

A fine day on a stretch of the Clyde that passes along Glasgow Green

you may see them out practising, from the boathouses on the bank. The Glasgow Humane Society have rescued many hundreds of people from the river over the years—and have had the sad task of recovering the bodies of those who have drowned. They have been on this site for more than 80 years.

At the far side of the Green, turn left.

7 TEMPLETON BUSINESS CENTRE

Facing you across the main carriageway to the People's Palace is the extraordinary façade of the Templeton Business Centre. The building was designed on the style of the Doge's Palace in Venice. During its construction in 1889 part of it collapsed, killing 29 women working in weaving sheds below. It was finally finished in 1892. At that time it was a carpet works. It has been recently refurbished to provide office accommodation.

Walk along the main carriageway to the People's Palace.

8 THE PEOPLE'S PALACE

This dates from the same period (1898) but is in rather more traditional style, an imposing building in red sandstone. The façade is decorated with allegorical

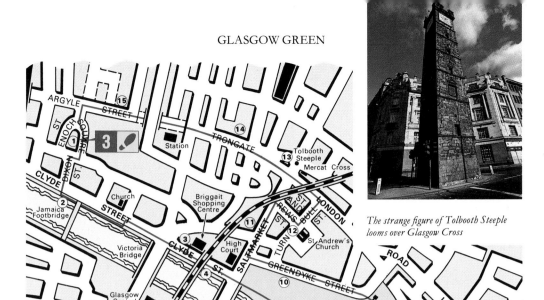

The strange figure of Tolbooth Steeple looms over Glasgow Cross

figures carved by a Glaswegian sculptor, Kellock Brown, and around the building are old lamp standards with the names of the Glasgow boroughs on them.

The museum inside is devoted to the history of the city and people of Glasgow. The Winter Gardens to the rear, all soaring ironwork and glass, have recently been refurbished.

Leaving the People's Palace, bear left to keep on the Green and go half right through a massive arch to join Greendyke Street.

9   THE ARCH
The carriageway outside the palace is the scene every September of the finish of the Glasgow Marathon. Numbers taking part have been as high as 11,000. The huge arch you walk through was 'presented to his fellow citizens by Bailie James McLennan JP' a century ago.

Walk down Greendyke Street and at the lights turn right into the Saltmarket.

10   GREENDYKE STREET
The church here, St-Andrew's-by-the-Green, the oldest Episcopal church in Scotland, was built in 1751, but was closed for worship in 1975. Across the road as you reach Saltmarket is the City Mortuary. It is open 24 hours a day and deals with up to 2,000 sudden deaths every year.

Walk up Saltmarket.

11   SALTMARKET
This was once the market handling the salt used for curing fish from the Clyde and the sea beyond.

Turn right into St Andrews Street.

12   ST ANDREW'S CHURCH
Facing you as you walk down St Andrews Street is another St Andrew's Church, a fine building dating from 1756. Its church organ was built by James Watt.

Turn left into Turnbull Street and left again into London Road to reach Glasgow Cross.

13   GLASGOW CROSS
This is the heart of the old city. The high Tolbooth Steeple is all that remains of the original 1626 building, erected at the point where

The Linen Bleachers, 1878, by Stephen Adam, in the People's Palace

people entered the city and paid their toll. The Mercat Cross with its unicorn marks the site of the first Glasgow market, dating back at least to 1175. Here, too, there was once a gallows.

Continue straight ahead along Trongate.

14   TRONGATE
Trongate was originally known as St Thenew's Gate, the name being changed when the Tron, or weighbridge, was set up. All Scottish burgh towns had a tron to weigh produce or carters' loads coming in.

Continue on along Argyle Street.

15   ARGYLE STREET
This street was named after Archibald, Duke of Argyle, a Scots nobleman. When he died in 1761 his body lay in state at the Highland Society House in Argyle Street.

Reach St Enoch Square and the finish of the walk.

A Learning Curve

*T*his walk explores the western end of the city, taking in Glasgow University, two fine museums, a pleasant park, a riverside walkway, the BBC and an extraordinary glass palace.

Glasgow University's neo-classical quadrangle designed by Gilbert Scott

3 miles/5km
Allow 2 hours

The walk starts at Hillhead Underground Station in Byres Road. On leaving the station, turn left and walk down Byres Road, turning left again into University Avenue at the lights.

1 BYRES ROAD
Formerly this led to a small settlement at its southern end called the Byres (cowsheds) of Partick. The area was developed in the late 19th century and is a fashionable part of Glasgow to this day. Hillhead has been the constituency of Roy Jenkins, one of the founders of the Social Democratic Party.

Walk up University Avenue to the university gatehouse at the top of the hill.

2 UNIVERSITY AVENUE
The establishment of Glasgow University dates from 1451, and it moved to the present site on Gilmorehill in 1870. The main campus buildings of that date were all designed by Sir George Gilbert Scott at a cost of £190,000. More recently the university has spread north and west in order to cope with the increased number of students.

The tall tower on the left as you walk up University Avenue is the Boyd Orr Building, opened in 1972 and named after a former chancellor of the university and Nobel Peace Prize winner. It is today used for science teaching. At the junction with University Place you are between Botany (right) and Mathematics (left). Continue to the gatehouse on the right at the top of the hill. To the left here is the modern library, the third phase of which was opened only in 1986, and the round Reading Room, a 1939 design by T Harred Hughes and D S K Waugh.

Enter the campus by the gatehouse and walk round the main block of buildings in an anticlockwise direction (ie bearing left), leaving by the Pearce Lodge to rejoin University Avenue.

3 GLASGOW UNIVERSITY
Take your time exploring the university. During normal office hours the information office at No.2 Professors' Square (first right on entering the quad) will supply a very good general guide to the university. It includes a map. The gatehouse also has a map available.

There is not room here to do more than outline some of the things to be seen within the university. The lamps around the square where you enter are all original and there is a Victorian pillar box still in use. On the left in the centre of the main block is the chapel, which dates back to 1928.

Beside the chapel is the Lion and Unicorn Staircase, which dates from 1690 and was moved here from the 'Old College' in the city. Turning left through a gateway brings you to the university's main frontage, with a fine view out over the city. It is possible to get an even better view by climbing the tower but permission must be obtained in advance (telephone 339 8855 extension 4271). The tower was completed by Gilbert Scott's son, Oldrid, in 1888, with the addition of an open spire.

A little further along the main frontage is Lord Kelvin's sundial. Turn left round the James Watt Building, a 1902 design by Sir John James Burnet, and walk down the drive to leave the campus at Pearce Lodge. The building dates originally from 1656 and was re-erected here in 1888 through a gift from the shipbuilder, Sir William Pearce. Over the gateway are the initials CRII indicating King Charles II, the reigning monarch at the time of the original construction. The Hunterian Museum in the main building tells the history of the university and also houses the magnificent collection of coins assembled by William Hunter (1718–83), a Glasgow graduate.

On rejoining University Avenue, walk back up the hill a short way to see the Memorial Gates.

4 MEMORIAL GATES
These were placed here in 1951 as part of the university's quincentenary celebrations. They bear the names of 28 famous graduates including Kelvin, Lister, Adam Smith and James Watt.

Walk back down University Avenue and turn right into Kelvin Way. At a path on the right, make a short diversion to pass two statues and bear left to rejoin Kelvin Way. Cross the river and turn right into the grounds of Kelvingrove Art Gallery and Museum.

5 KELVIN WAY
Among the many fine trees on this leafy avenue is an oak, not far from University Avenue, that was planted in 1918 to mark the granting of votes to women. The short diversion down the path takes you past statues of Lord Kelvin and Lord Lister. Kelvin was one of the pioneers of the use of electricity and Lister did much to further the use of antiseptics in medicine. The more modern sculpture nearer the river, by Benno Schotz, commemorates Dr Tom Honeyman, Rector of the university from 1953 to 1956.

On the bridge over the River Kelvin are four groups of statuary, erected in 1926. They represent respectively Commerce and Industry, Peace and War, Navigation and Shipping, and Progress and Prosperity.

Walk round to the front of the art gallery.

6 ART GALLERY AND MUSEUM
This collection is open every day and admission is free. It contains many fine paintings and other displays of interest in what is claimed to be one of the best municipal art collections in Britain.

Leave the art gallery by the main entrance. Turn left into Argyle Street and left again back into Kelvin Way. Cross the road and enter Kelvingrove Park.

7 KELVIN HALL
This hall, which stands opposite as you join Argyle Street, has been used for many and varied events including world championship boxing, circuses and exhibitions. In March 1985 it underwent a dramatic transformation in order to stage the world curling championships. In a period of 10 days, miles of piping were laid and an ice rink was created. From 1988 it will house the Transport Museum.

The next section of the walk is happily traffic-free. At the first junction of paths go ahead and slightly left. Take the next path left and keep to the right of the large fountain. Past the fountain, cut across the grass, bearing right for a few yards to join a path heading uphill.

8 THE FOUNTAIN

On the left just after the first path junction is a tree planted to mark the opening of Glasgow's first Skateboard Centre here in March 1978. It seems to have been a short-lived craze for one rarely sees skateboards nowadays.

The massive fountain is yet another example of the Victorians commemorating in monuments the great and the good. This one was erected in honour of Robert Stewart, Lord Provost of Glasgow 1851–4 'to whose unwearied exertions the citizens are indebted for the abundant water supply from Loch Katrine'.

The fountain was placed here in 1872 and Lord Provost Stewart would no doubt be happy to know that Glasgow still takes water from Loch Katrine in the Trossachs, some 30 miles to the north of Glasgow.

As you walk uphill you pass a curious statue depicting a lion with an eagle in its mouth.

At cross-paths keep straight on uphill to join the broad upper path. Follow it to the large equestrian statue ahead.

9 THE ROBERTS EQUESTRIAN STATUE

The statue is of Field Marshal Earl Roberts of Kandahar, a great soldier who died in France in November 1914. Seated on his horse, he has a fine view over to the university and across the park. Kelvingrove Park's 85 green acres were acquired by the city in 1852. Apart from the skateboard park, it has a duck pond and a large children's play area, but most of all it is used for quiet recreation. It is especially popular with people working in the offices round about as a fine place for a lunchtime break.

Past the Roberts statue, turn left downhill. Keeping within the park, twist downhill (there are several ways down) to reach the lowest path, beside the river. Go through a tunnel under the road to reach the gardens and car park by Kelvinbridge. Keeping close to the river, go under the bridge and continue on the Kelvin Walkway.

10 KELVINBRIDGE

After wet weather the river thunders through this stretch in impressive style. On the bridge is the coat of arms of the City of Glasgow with its motto 'Let Glasgow Flourish'. (The full motto is 'Lord, let Glasgow flourish by the preaching of the Word and praising thy Name'.) The coat of arms was granted to the city by Lord Lyon in 1866.

After walking under another road bridge, cross the river by a pleasant footbridge. After passing the ruins of a former building—possibly a mill—pass a weir. In another 50 yards take the path on the right to climb up to the road. Turn left at the top of the steps and left again at Queen Margaret Drive to cross the river.

11 BBC SCOTLAND

The Kelvin Walkway continues out to Milngavie, where, by joining the West Highland Way path, it is possible to walk all the way to Fort William, a distance of about 100 miles! Ahead and left, as you cross the river on Queen Margaret Drive, are the headquarters of BBC Scotland. There is a marked contrast between the original building at this end of the block, with its imposing and somehow very solemn façade, and the extension at the other end built recently in much more functional style. Both radio and television programmes are recorded and transmitted from here.

Cross the road by the BBC and enter the Botanic Gardens. After walking round the gardens, leave by the main entrance in the south-east corner on to Great Western Road.

12 BOTANIC GARDENS

Open daily, they include large glasshouses and conservatories displaying many fascinating plants from all over the world. The development of gardens on this site started in 1842 through the Royal Botanical Institute of Glasgow. Their acquisition by the city, which has turned out so happily, occurred through misfortune. The Institute raised a substantial loan in 1883 to pay for the new range of glasshouses. They ran into difficulties repaying the loan and in 1887 Glasgow Corporation took the gardens over as creditors. The City of Glasgow Act in 1891 included a clause transferring ownership and responsibility for the Botanic Gardens to the city, they are now safe for all time.

The glory of the gardens has to be the Kibble Palace, a fantastic glass structure dating from 1873 containing a unique collection of tree ferns and plants from temperate areas. As well as its plant displays, it encloses nine sculptures—each by a different artist—the subjects including Eve, Cain, Ruth and, in delightful contrast, King Robert of Sicily. A guide to the gardens is available on site.

On leaving the gardens, cross Great Western Road (take great care, it is very busy with traffic) and walk down Byres Road back to Hillhead Underground Station and the end of a fascinating walk.

Pollok Park

*T**his walk explores the splendid Pollok Country Park, truly a piece
of the countryside within the city. Much of the way is wooded or beside the
White Cart river. Most of the paths have excellent surfaces but one or two
short stretches may be muddy after wet weather. The walk is virtually
traffic-free.*

Pollok Country Park is situated 3
miles south-west of Glasgow city
centre, as shown in the map
above. A leaflet giving details of
its attractions and an overall plan
of the park is available from the
Countryside Rangers' Centre,
Pollok House, and the Burrell
Collection in the park, and also
from the Greater Glasgow Tourist
Board, 35–39 St Vincent Place.

---

*3¼ miles/6km
Allow 2 hours*

---

*The walk starts and finishes at the car
park outside the splendid new building
housing the magnificent Burrell
Collection. If using public transport,
take one of the frequent trains from
Glasgow Central to Pollokshaws West
and join the walk at Shawmuir Lodge,
the main entrance to the park.*

*Leave the Burrell (of which more
later) by the surfaced path going east
along the edge of the large field. Take the
first path on the left, and at the fork
keep left to walk up through a strip of
woodland. At the junction of paths
opposite the top end of the large field on
the left, turn right to cross a small
footbridge; then take the left-hand path
up through the woods to emerge on a road.
Turn left here on the surfaced path
(minor road but not open to the public).*

1 NORTH LODGE
Pollok Park was given to the city of
Glasgow by the Maxwell family in
1966, and was designated as a
Country Park by the Countryside
Commission for Scotland in 1980. It
covers about 370 acres and contains
much of interest, not least the
wildlife, which includes roe deer,
foxes, rabbits and a wide variety of
birds—magpies, thrushes,
blackbirds, tits, goldcrests and
treecreepers. The splendid
woodland is a feature of the park:
there are fine horse chestnuts, elms,

yews, oaks, beech and birch.

On the right as you emerge on to
the surfaced path is the North
Lodge, built in 1892. It is one of five
such lodges guarding the entrances
to the park. Just to the left of the
surfaced path is a track, now
somewhat hidden and often muddy.
It is part of a long avenue planted by
Sir John Stirling Maxwell just a
century ago, in 1887, and featuring
many fine lime trees. In April the
area is a mass of daffodils.

*Follow the surfaced path to the top of
the gentle rise.*

2 FORT
On the right here is the outline of an
old fortification, with banks and
ditches, dating back to medieval
times. These fortlets were generally
erected as observation posts, hence
the placement on the highest
ground.

*Take the first path on the left after
the fort and, always bearing right, walk
round the Fish Pond to rejoin the main
path.*

3 FISH POND
On the pond you may see
waterfowl. In summer there are
dragonflies and damselflies
hovering over the water, which
itself contains a fascinating
assortment of life, from frogs and
toads to water scorpions and pond
skaters. A leaflet is available from
the Park Rangers' Office.

*Keep on the main path as it curves left,
then right to pass the Glade. The path
eventually crosses an open space with
picnic tables.*

*View of the sawmill and battery house by
the weir in the White Cart Water*

4 THE GLADE
This is a delightful grassy area
shaded by trees. If you are lucky you
might catch a glimpse of a roe deer,
its white rump standing out as it
moves through the trees. In autumn
this is a good place for toadstools,
and there are many woodland birds
here all year round. On your left in
the open area past the Glade are
three fine turkey oaks, one of which
has a holly bush sprouting from its
base. Some of the young horse
chestnuts may have bark damage
caused by roe deer marking their
territory.

*Follow the path as it bends sharply
left to go downhill to Pollok House.*

5 POLLOK HOUSE
Pollok was the home of the Maxwell
family for over 600 years. The house
we see today is believed to be the
fourth on the site; it was begun in
1747 with additional wings and
terraces added between 1890 and
1908. The house is open for viewing
every day and entrance is free. The
facilities include a café and toilets.

*At the crossroads outside Pollok
House turn sharp right, following the
signs for the Demonstration Garden.*

6 THE BRIDGE
The walk along towards the
Demonstration Garden is beside the
White Cart river. The very attractive
bridge over the river was built in
1757 (one of the centrestones bears
this date) and its parapets carry 40

curved balusters on each side.

Opposite the bridge, set into the wall, is a memorial to 58 officers and men 'from the tenantry and staff of Nether Pollok' who served in World War I. Twelve of them did not return. The numbers give an indication of the size of the estate at that time—it would probably have employed about 200 people in all.

Follow the path as it curves right of the stable block.

7   THE WEIR
The stable block is late 18th century.

Before reaching the Rangers' Office you will see a weir in the river. It served the sawmill which is also to be seen. Timber was harvested from the estate on quite a large scale in the 19th and early 20th century. A battery house beside the sawmill provided electricity for the estate, including the 'big house', by 1900. Sir John Stirling Maxwell, who was resident here at that time, was passionately interested in forestry and carried out many field trials to establish new varieties of trees in Scotland.

Pass the Rangers' Office.

8   RANGERS' OFFICE
This was formerly a small chapel. Inside is a wide range of very interesting leaflets about many aspects of the park. The rangers are always pleased to talk to visitors, and they organise regular guided walks within the park.

Continue to the Demonstration Garden.

9   DEMONSTRATION GARDEN
This is a quite fascinating two acres which should not be missed. Displays include border plants, vegetables, fruit, trees and shrubs. There are rose, heather, alpine and butterfly gardens, a heated glasshouse and even a plant board where 'garden draughts' can be played. The original gardeners' 'bothy' has been restored to give an idea of how the gardener lived 100 years ago.

On leaving the Demonstration Garden, rejoin the path beside the White Cart.

10   WHITE CART RIVERBANK
There is interest on either side along this riverbank walk. On the water are mallards and moorhens. The willow trees overhanging the river provide food for small birds in the winter. Further along, the giant hogweed plant grows up to 12ft (3½m) high. Believe it or not, it is a member of the carrot family. DO NOT TOUCH IT: the sap is poisonous and can cause very nasty skin blisters.

The first field on the left—known as the Shinty Field—often houses some of the park's fine herd of Highland cattle. There are about 50 in all within the park, including two bulls, and they have won many prizes at shows over the years.

The second field is used for training police dogs, and some of the apparatus can be seen in the field. Strathclyde Police have 60 dogs in all, mostly German Shepherds but with a small number of labradors which are used for sniffing out explosives and drugs. On Tuesday mornings between 10.30 and 11.30 the public can enjoy demonstrations of the agility and obedience of these beautiful animals.

The third field is the very attractive home of Poloc Cricket Club. Some people may not associate Scotland with cricket, but the game has a very long history north of the Border.

Pass tennis courts and a car park and bear right by the river to reach the road near the main park entrance.

11   SHAWMUIR LODGE
Opposite the tennis courts are the metal supports of a former suspension bridge across the river. It was closed in the 1960s when it became unsafe. On the right as you reach the road is Shawmuir Lodge, dating, like the North Lodge, from the 1890s. This is the main vehicular entrance to the park.

Turn left along the road for about 50yds (walk on the right to face the traffic) and then turn right along a path signposted to the Burrell Collection. Follow this path as it crosses a ditch by a footbridge and return to the start of the walk by going half left across the open field. The Burrell Collection building is in front of you.

12   THE BURRELL COLLECTION
Both the building itself and its contents have won awards since opening in 1983. The collection was left to the city by Sir William Burrell with the condition that it be housed in a rural setting, and providing a home for the Burrell was in the mind of Mrs Anne Maxwell Macdonald when she gifted Pollok Park to Glasgow in 1966.

The Burrell Collection is open every day, admission is free (though there is a charge for car parking) and facilities include a café and a shop.

Left: this formal garden featuring box hedging and planted terrace walls adjoins Pollok House. Below: main entrance to the Burrell Collection

A Canal Ramble

This most unusual and interesting linear walk follows the final stretch of the former Forth and Clyde Canal into Glasgow. The towpath provides an excellent walking surface throughout and is of course perfectly flat (except for the short climb past Maryhill Locks).

large numbers of people who left here for Botany Bay in Australia, were once a centre for shipbuilding, turning out many of the famous Clyde 'puffers'. The 16 lock gates at Maryhill are being replaced as part of the project to reopen the canal for navigation. The gates, weighing seven tons each, are being made in the Scottish Maritime Museum at

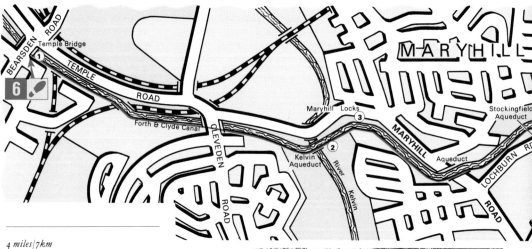

4 miles/7km
Allow 2 hours

The walk starts at Temple Bridge, where the A809 road to Bearsden crosses the canal (half a mile north of Anniesland Cross, which is reached by taking the A82 from the city centre). If using public transport, there are frequent bus services to Anniesland Cross from the city centre and it is only a few minutes' walk to Temple Bridge.

Join the canal at Temple Bridge by the Lock 27 restaurant and bar and head towards the city, with the canal on your left. Before reaching the first road crossing, you go over two sets of railway lines and pass another lock.

1 TEMPLE BRIDGE

The Forth and Clyde Canal was a principal throughroute for both passengers and freight for over a century. It was first opened in 1777 and was finally completed in 1790, linking Grangemouth on the Forth to Bowling Basin, near Dumbarton on the Clyde; in 1822 a link with the Union Canal, which ran all the way into Edinburgh, was opened in Falkirk.

The canal was closed to navigation in 1963 but in recent years much work has been carried out to improve both the waterway itself and the paths alongside it. You can now take short boat cruises at several points and the canal offers splendid traffic-free walking opportunities, one of which— perhaps the most dramatic—you are just starting.

Cross Cleveden Road and rejoin the towpath. The area ahead is known as Maryhill, with the houses on the distinct hilltop. At a path junction keep left to cross the Kelvin Aqueduct.

A lovely spot for a fisherman and his dog on the Forth and Clyde Canal

2 KELVIN AQUEDUCT

This really is a wonderful piece of city canalscape. The Kelvin Aqueduct is 70ft (21m) high and its four arches carry the canal for 400ft (122m) over the river below. (Turning right here would take you on to the Kelvin Walkway, used in Walk 4.) It is worth making a short diversion to the right in fact, the better to appreciate the graceful architecture of the aqueduct. It dates, like the canal, from 1790. When it opened it was the largest aqueduct of its kind in Britain.

Continue up through the five Maryhill Locks.

3 MARYHILL LOCKS

Both the Kelvin Aqueduct and the Maryhill Locks are now happily listed as scheduled ancient monuments. The locks, known locally as the Botany because of the

Irvine, Ayrshire, and it is hoped to have them in place by 1990.

At the top of the locks the towpath continues, soon swinging left with the canal to cross Maryhill Road.

4 STOCKINGFIELD AQUEDUCT

The aqueduct across Maryhill Road was rebuilt in 1881. About 500yds past it is the Stockingfield Aqueduct, carrying the canal across Lochburn Road. This one is still original. It was built by Robert Whitworth, who took over from John Smeaton as the canal's chief engineer.

At Stockingfield Junction keep on the same towpath to follow the Glasgow Branch of the canal.

5 THE GLASGOW BRANCH

A bridge at the junction bears a plate informing you that you have 2½ miles to go to reach Port Dundas. This may be somewhat of an overestimate, but on such a splendid path it hardly matters. Around here you will generally see birds on the canal—swans and coots for example. The canal going left here is the main Forth and Clyde, heading out of the city. Up to now you have been on the Forth and Clyde but you now walk beside the Glasgow Branch, which took traffic to Port Dundas, under a mile from the city centre.

Continue on the towpath to cross Ruchill Street.

6   RUCHILL PARISH CHURCH

On the right about 200yds past the canal junction is a spillway, used for controlling the water level by carrying off surplus water.

The large church over to the right is Ruchill Parish Church. Its modest-looking hall was, surprisingly, designed by Charles Rennie Mackintosh. It is of grey sandstone and actually predates the church. It was opened in 1898 and is, by Mackintosh standards, a fairly

Cross Church, another Mackintosh building. It is now the headquarters of the Charles Rennie Mackintosh Society and offers regular lectures and exhibitions associated with the life and work of Mackintosh.

A more recent addition to the scene is a fine geometric mural on a house wall.

Cross Firhill Road and pass to the right of the basin to rejoin the towpath in about 400yds.

8   FIRHILL BASIN

This was originally associated with the timber trade. It is sometimes used nowadays for canoeing. On the right is Firhill Park, the home of Partick Thistle Football Club. They are known to their supporters as the Jags. The ground is shared with Clyde FC.

Continue along the towpath—recently upgraded to provide an excellent walking surface—to Hamiltonhill Basin.

9   HAMILTONHILL BASIN

The basin was the terminus of this branch of the canal when it was first opened. There is a connection with Walk 5 in that Sir William Burrell once owned a shipyard here.

Across a neat footbridge are the new offices of the British Waterways Board and the Forth and Clyde Canal Project Officer. Information on the canal is available during

working hours.

The stretch of canal just walked gives grand views into the heart of Glasgow, and it must have been a singularly pleasant experience to reach the city this way. Let us hope that one day the Forth and Clyde at Hamiltonhill will again see working boats passing through.

Cross Possil Road by another aqueduct and walk down to the end of the canal at Port Dundas.

10   PORT DUNDAS

After crossing Possil Road you pass through a rather run-down area, but keep going, for there is better ahead. The canal curves right and left to reveal the magnificent North Spiers Wharf buildings, a very fine group of Victorian warehouses. They once housed sugar and grain but are now used as a whisky bond, storing spirit under the aegis of the Customs and Excise. The rather smaller building at the end of the group was built in 1812 as the canal company's office.

It is hard to imagine getting on a boat here bound for Edinburgh, but that used to be the case. The place is named after Lord Dundas, one of the partners in the canal venture, who cut the first sod of turf for its building 200 years ago.

The walk can be extended slightly by crossing Craighall Road and turning into North Canalbank Street.

11   NORTH CANALBANK STREET

On the right here was the Port Dundas basin, opened in 1791 and not cut off from the rest of the canal until the 1960s. Also here was a further junction, with the Monklands Canal. The latter is now piped and feeds about two million gallons of water into the Forth and Clyde each day.

There are two ways of returning to Temple Bridge. From Garscube Road near Port Dundas you can catch a bus (service 21 or 60) to Maryhill Locks, and walk the short way back to the start. Or why not simply turn round and walk back? The views are quite different going the other way and a very satisfying 8-mile (13km) outing can be made.

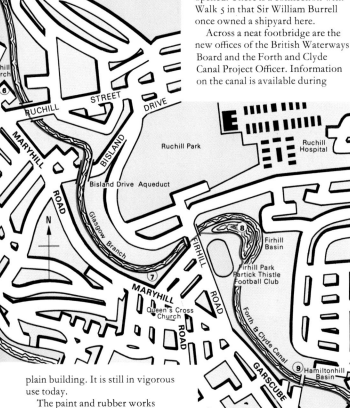

plain building. It is still in vigorous use today.

The paint and rubber works across the canal each originally had their own wharf for loading and unloading goods. The tall chimney on the right of the canal just past Ruchill Street serves East Park children's home.

Continue across Bilsland Drive Aqueduct to swing left and right and reach Firhill Road.

7   QUEEN'S CROSS CHURCH

As the canal swings left there is a pleasant view ahead of the trees and open spaces of Ruchill Park. On the right, at the junction of Garscube Road and Maryhill Road, is Queen's

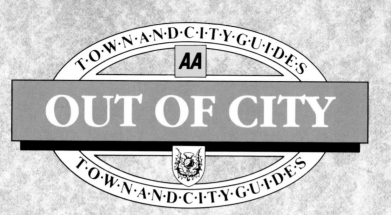

OUT OF CITY

T·O·W·N·A·N·D·C·I·T·Y·G·U·I·D·E·S

AA

T·O·W·N·A·N·D·C·I·T·Y·G·U·I·D·E·S

A great advantage of Glasgow is that it is so easy to get out of the city—to the lovely country estate of Greenbank Gardens, for instance

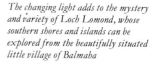

The changing light adds to the mystery and variety of Loch Lomond, whose southern shores and islands can be explored from the beautifully situated little village of Balmaha

BALDERNOCK

99 NS 5775

On a hillside rising from the valley of the Kelvin, this is an old-fashioned parish of farms and country houses linked by narrow, meandering and often none too well-surfaced minor roads.

The isolated parish church of 1795 figured as 'Lintiehaugh Kirk' in Graham Moffat's still faintly remembered smash-hit Scottish comedy *Bunty Pulls the Strings*, which had a record 16-month run in 1911–12 at the Haymarket Theatre in London. In 1932, Queen Mary asked for the play to be revived for a Royal Charity Matinée, at which she was noticed whispering to a baffled Duchess of Devonshire translations of such Scotticisms as 'peelie-wallie', still a familiar word for somebody pale and unwell.

Baldernock also has a fine golf course at Balmore, a tree-fringed loch used by dinghy-sailors at Bardowie, and a demonstration garden with flowerbeds, heathers and a rockpool at Torrance, the village at its south-eastern tip.

After an embattled history, Bothwell Castle stands ruined but still splendid, one of the largest and finest stone castles in Scotland

BALLOCH

99 NS 3981

Dinghies and motor-cruisers cram the riverside at this little town through which the River Leven drains Loch Lomond to the Clyde. A stroll down the Leven towpath leads to the unobtrusive barrage which is almost the only clue that this magnificent, world-famous loch doubles as a reservoir.

Balloch's boatyards are the starting-point for short cruises around the wooded islands at the southern end. Full-length cruises by the *Countess Fiona* leave from Balloch Pier, which is, confusingly, some distance away.

Footpaths and a driveway lead into Balloch Castle Country Park, which sweeps up a hillside with woodland trails, a tucked-away walled garden and sloping picnic lawns with gorgeous views over the loch.

Overlooking the picnic lawns, battlemented Balloch Castle is an architectural hoax of 1808. Its visitor centre concentrates on local history and wildlife. Illustrations take the form of stained-glass panels, three-dimensional glass paintings and, very effectively, real-life views through the castle windows.

BALMAHA

99 NS 4290

Geology and centuries of woodland management have combined to give this little village on the east shore of Loch Lomond a most beautiful situation. The Highland Boundary Fault has created a series of rounded, descending summits above Balmaha. It continues as a line of wooded islands, and disappears from view at Ben Bowie on the south-western skyline.

Forest walks here include a gentle stroll through spruce plantations and a stiff climb through larchwoods to some spectacular viewpoints. Long-distance walkers also come through, as they tackle the West Highland Way to Fort William.

Across a bay, the steep and tangled woodlands of the island of Inchcailloch look almost impenetrable. But there is a fascinating 2½-mile (4km) nature trail through coppiced oakwoods once harvested on a 24-year cycle, pine, alder and holly; past a burial ground first used in the 8th century and the ruins of a parish church where the mainland folk worshipped until 1621. Fallow deer have been settled on Inchcailloch for 650 years.

Visitors to Inchcailloch are ferried across from the boatyard at Balmaha, which is also the starting-point for the mail-boat cruise round all the inhabited islands in the loch.

BEARSDEN

99 NS 5471

A notorious trap for unwary newsreaders, the name of this dormitory town on the edge of Glasgow is pronounced as if it did have a wild-animal connection; but it probably derives from 'bere'—a kind of barley.

Bearsden was on the northern frontier of the Roman Empire. Two well-preserved stretches of the foundations of the coast-to-coast Antonine Wall, built about AD142, survive in the hilltop cemetery. Near the town centre, beside Roman Road, the remains of a bath-house were discovered in 1973, and are now carefully labelled to show where the hot and cold rooms, changing rooms and furnace were located.

Bearsden has two pleasant little lochs within its boundaries: St Germains in a lightly wooded hollow with villa gardens sloping down to it, and Kilmardinny in a small public park. Above it,

Kilmardinny House is a Georgian mansion now flourishing as an arts centre. The fine interior features a first-floor gallery with a splendid ornate dome.

BISHOPBRIGGS

100 NS 6070
This mostly 20th-century town on Glasgow's northern edge is well supplied with sports facilities. Huntershill Recreation Centre is based on the boyhood mansion-house home of Thomas Muir, a lawyer and famous political reformer. He was sentenced at a show trial in 1793 to transportation to Botany Bay, but made an adventurous escape from there to Revolutionary France.One room is now a Thomas Muir museum.

When 'Bishop's-bridge' was just a cluster of weavers' cottages, what is now the nearby conservation hamlet of Cadder was the population centre of the district. Set beside a bridge over the Forth and Clyde Canal, it is a popular place for canal-boat cruises from Kirkintilloch (see page 84) and has a lightly wooded, winding towpath walk.

There has been a church here for 800 years, but the present building dates only from the 1820s, a decade when people were very nervous about body-snatchers. Cadder Kirk retains a sturdy watch-house in its graveyard, and a cast-iron mort-safe, placed over newly arrived coffins until their contents were no longer of any interest to the Resurrectionists.

Blantyre's David Livingstone Centre— museum and national memorial to the 19th-century missionary and explorer

BLANTYRE

100 NS 6857
Visitors from all over the world come to this one-time cotton-mill town to see the David Livingstone Centre, Scotland's national memorial to the great African missionary–explorer, who was born here in 1813.

Livingstone was brought up in a single-roomed house in Shuttle Row above the River Clyde, and the whole block of 24 houses has been restored as a museum which provides an imaginative self-guided tour of splendid exhibits. These include the history of the town; Livingstone's life and schooldays here; his work in Africa; his journeys of exploration and the intense interest in them back in Victorian Britain; the famous 'Dr Livingstone, I presume?' meeting with Henry Stanley; and that final journey, after his death, when his African companions carried his body 1,500 miles (2,410km) to the coast.

The centre is set among lawns and gardens, and modern Africa is not forgotten. In the Africa Pavilion, the story is continued from Livingstone's time right up to the present day.

BOTHWELL

100 NS 7058
A fine Victorian parish church here contains many elements of its 12th- and 14th-century predecessors. At Bothwell Bridge there is a monument commemorating the battle of 1679 when a stunning defeat was suffered by the over-confident Covenanters.

But the historic glory of the town is the mellow sandstone ruin of Bothwell Castle on a high grassy bank at a wooded curve of the River Clyde.

It was besieged, defended and partly demolished several times during the Scottish-English wars, but in its heyday Bothwell was a stronghold of an Earl of Douglas known, from his demeanour in battle, as Archibald the Grim. He completed the handsome curtain walls.

Bothwell Castle is an Ancient Monument. A Duke of Buccleuch came to admire it in 1786, leaving his initial and a ducal coronet carved beside a basement well.

The Clyde is a major attraction for visitors to the region, flowing as it does through some of the loveliest countryside in Scotland—here the Clyde Valley at Rosebank

CLYDE MUIRSHIEL REGIONAL PARK

98NS3163
Occupying more than 30,000 acres of moorland, river valleys, coastline and lochs, Clyde Muirshiel is a mixture of public and privately owned land which caters for a remarkable variety of interests, from bird-watching and water sports to industrial archaeology and exhilarating walks.

There are ranger-staffed visitor centres at several key locations. One which combines many of the park's special interests is at Cornalees Bridge above Inverkip. The Kip Water flows from the nearby reservoir of Loch Thom, named after the brilliant civil engineer Robert Thom who devised the series of reservoirs, sluices and water channels—locally called cuts—which supplied the once flourishing industries of Greenock.

Thom's system opened in 1827, went out of use only in 1971, and is now preserved as an industrial monument. Inside the Cornalees Bridge Centre, visitors can see a re-created section of the main Greenock Cut, and are then invited to go outside to the real thing, perhaps to tackle a fine 5-mile (8km) walk which provides superb views over the Firth of Clyde.

There is a major display on the Greenock Cut, but Cornalees is also a wildlife information centre. After tumbling down the sluices from Loch Thom, the Kip Water flows through the steep-sided Shieldhill Glen. A nature trail goes deep into the glen, where roe deer browse in protected woodlands of ash and oak, rowan and birch.

A picnic site above the glen is on the base of an old wartime gun emplacement; the view out to sea, which was useful to the gunners, is just another attraction of the peaceful Shieldhill of today.

The visitor centre that is situated higher than any of the others in the park is at Muirshiel, in the heart of what was once a private estate in the wild and Highland-like upper glen of the River Calder. Mixed deciduous woodlands, conifer plantations and rhododendron thickets gone wild provide shelter for Muirshiel's nature trails; but all around, the view is to bare heathery grouse moors.

Different patches of the moorland are burned each year as part of a management plan to provide fresh growth for the grouse and the sheep which also graze the moors. Hill walkers often start excursions from Muirshiel, but they know that

summits like Misty Law did not come by their names casually.

Muirshiel is fine bird-watching territory, since its varied habitats attract species as different as goldcrests in the woodland, buzzards and sparrowhawks over the open moor, and dippers walking along underwater as they feed on the riverbed.

Castle Semple Water Park near Lochwinnoch is on lower ground and provides a very different range of activities. Sailing, rowing, canoeing and sailboarding are all popular here, and there is coarse fishing for roach and perch and some forbidding pike.

Other parts of the park include an inland picnic area at Barnbrock Farm between Lochwinnoch and Kilmacolm, and a coastal stretch at Lunderston Bay where there are more picnic areas beside a sand and shingle beach.

CARRON VALLEY

100NS7082
Close to its source, the River Carron is dammed to create a reservoir in a valley between forested hills. Overlooking the north end, a grassy picnic place stands beside the site of Sir John de Graham's 13th-century castle, a flat-topped mound defended by a ditch where rushes, irises and marsh marigolds grow. Further down the valley, a roadside enclosure round a graveyard is all that remains of the ancient Kirk O'Muir; but an open-air church service is still held here every summer.

Near the dam, Spittal Bridge picnic site is on a little river island. Forest walks head up through the conifers, one soon turning off to a children's adventure playground. Twice a year, the main forest roads here are used by rally cars.

CHATELHERAULT

100 NS7353
There is a simple explanation for the
exotic name of this splendid country
park opened in 1987. It is centred on
the very ornate hilltop shooting
lodge created by William Adam in
the 1730s for the Duke of Hamilton.
The Hamiltons are also Dukes of
Chatelherault in France, and the
lodge echoes a French design.

It contains some of the finest
Thomas Clayton plasterwork,
recently restored at a very high cost.
A visitor centre in the walled garden
tells the history of the Hamiltons
and the estate.

So close to the industrial belt of
Scotland, it is a great surprise to
come across the well-graded
footpaths beyond the house. These
wander along the thickly wooded
margins of the deep and winding
Avon Gorge.

CLYDE VALLEY

99 NS8246
Below Lanark, the Clyde winds
from side to side of a narrow,
wooded and productive valley once
admired for its 'blossoming
orchards'. But apples like the
Cambusnethan Pippin, Jargonelle
pears, Orleans plums and Green
Gaskin gooseberries have largely
given way to a series of nurseries
and garden centres.

There are five riverside villages in
succession up the valley. Dalserf no
longer has the collection of inns
which served a ferry across the
Clyde, but retains its parish church
of 1655, with no fewer than four
outside stairways and a little
ornamental belfry. At Rosebank, the
mock-Tudor style of houses and a
hotel is thanks to the taste of an
estate owner of the 1880s. Crossford
has a wildlife reserve in the steep
Nethan Gorge and a road leading up
to historic Craignethan Castle.
Hazelbank has a narrow riverside
park sheltering among the pines.
And by the old weavers' village of
Kirkfieldbank, the twisting A72 is
ready for the steep climb on the far
side of the Clyde to Lanark.

COATBRIDGE

100 NS7265
Once the busiest iron-making town
in Scotland, Coatbridge has
managed to make a virtue out of
losing its staple industry.
Summerlee Heritage Park opened in
1987 on the site of a long-

*Chatelherault, the 18th-century hunting
lodge by William Adam*

demolished ironworks, and in a
programme of steady development
planned into the mid-1990s will
become one of the most
comprehensive industrial visitor
centres in Britain.

In a massive exhibition hall,
working machinery from iron- and
steelworks, heavy engineering
plants and coal-mines has been
installed. Outside, the plans call for
the building of an electric tramway
system round the 25-acre site.

The Summerlee Branch of the
Monkland Canal is to be reopened,
so that a modern replica of a horse-
drawn barge can take visitors along
the 3½ miles (5½km) of canal to
Drumpellier Country Park.

Drumpellier's information centre
is beside a loch stocked with brown
and rainbow trout, where mute
swans, mallard, coot, waterhen and
tufted duck are usually to be seen.
Nature trails spread out through
woodlands of oak and lime,
sycamore, maple, ash, horse
chestnut, beech and pine.

*Not a dinosaur—in Summerlee
Heritage Park's industrial visitor
centre—but a heavy steam crane from
Colville's iron- and steelworks in
Motherwell*

Palacerigg Country Park deer

CUMBERNAULD

100 NS 7676
Scotland's breeziest New Town,
established in 1956, is well known
for its separation of pedestrians and
traffic, for the garden-like
appearance of many of its individual
districts, and as the setting for Bill
Forsyth's film *Gregory's Girl*.

Totally different in surroundings
and atmosphere, the old village of
Cumbernauld still generally follows
its original 17th-century plan. Its
houses were built along a main
street from the parish church to the
castle, with long narrow gardens
behind.

Palacerigg Country Park lies on
the high-set moorland south-east of
the town. Its informative visitor
centre has displays on the varied
local wildlife, there is a children's
farm with collections of rare breeds
of farm animals, and the park also
includes a golf course, a sailing loch,
pony trails and several nature walks.

A waymarked walk past the
waterfall in the Glencryan Woods
passes the site of an old fireclay
mine. Fireclay deposits around
Palacerigg were worked from
Roman times until 1958.

The mine is the subject of a walk-
in display—with taped sound
effects—at the visitor centre, which
also has an exhibition on the
Palacerigg Colony. From 1907 to
1939 the moorland now occupied by
the park was a labour colony
worked by unemployed men who
were brought in their hundreds,
every weekday, by train from
Glasgow.

They raised crops, built roads and
a now-uplifted railway, reclaimed
land for cultivation and dug peat
which was turned into firelighters
and fuel.

CUMBRAE

98 NS 1757
Easily reached by car ferry from
Largs, Great Cumbrae is one of the
beautiful holiday islands in the Firth
of Clyde.

The village of Millport, spreading
round two miles of rocky coves and
sandy beaches, faces a cluster of
islets in a bay. Overlooking the main
sands, the Garrison—originally
built in the 1740s for the captain of a
revenue cutter—houses a museum
devoted to the main island and the
'Wee Cumbrae' nearby.

Travelled by generations of
holidaymakers on hired bicycles, the
$10\frac{1}{4}$-mile ($16\frac{1}{2}$km) round-island road
is very attractive as it passes the
Marine Biological Station at Keppel,
the towering Lion Rock formed
from much harder material than the
sandstone which has weathered
away around it, and the National
Water Sports Training Centre near
the ferry slip, before returning to
Millport past the west-facing sands
of Fintray Bay.

An 'inner circle' road climbs 417ft
(127m) to the superb viewpoint at
the Glaid Stane. On a fine evening,
though, the classic Millport view is
from the Farland Hills. Above the
twinkling lights of the town and of
the yachts and cruisers moored in
the bay, a fiery sun dips down
behind the hills of Bute and Kintyre.

DRYMEN

99 NS 4788
A residential village centred on a
square where the Clachan Inn dates
back to 1734, this place is actually
'Drimmen', despite the jocular
appearance of a trio of toby-jug
figures outside a hotel bar called the
Three Dry Men. The *druim* which
gave the village its name is the
Gaelic word for a ridge.

From the square, the Old
Gartmore Road, once a coaching
route towards the Trossachs, leads
through Garadhban Forest, where
waymarked walks give fine views of
Loch Lomond, and the long-
distance West Highland Way also
passes through.

South-east of Drymen, and again
on the West Highland Way,
Gartness is an old mill village now
little more than a row of red-
sandstone cottages above the
Endrick Water. On the east side of
the bridge there is access to the Pots
of Gartness, a series of falls much
visited in the autumn as salmon
battle up the rocky ledges.

DUMBARTON

99NS4075

Many of the offices of Strathclyde Regional Council are located in this town astride the River Leven, where it flows into the Clyde. But that is a minor distinction compared with its status 1,500 years ago when, as *Dun Breatann*—the Fort of the Britons— this was the capital of the independent Kingdom of Strathclyde.

The Britons' stronghold was not on the low riverside ground, but high on the twin-peaked volcanic plug called Dumbarton Rock, which had a military garrison until the early years of this century.

As it stands today, Dumbarton Castle is a series of mostly Georgian buildings at different levels on the Rock. Behind the Governor's House at the foot of the cliffs, a steep and narrow staircase between the two separated hills leads through the Portcullis Arch (probably 14th century) to the airy upper levels of grassy lawns and bare rock faces.

The French Prison is where captured Napoleonic soldiers were held, and, for safety, the magazine is the highest building of them all.

There are outstanding views from the upper part of the castle: from the Duke of Argyll's Battery, the Duke of York's Battery and the Prince of Wales Battery—all now serving as viewpoints—and from the highest point of all, the site of the White Tower on the western summit 240ft (73m) directly above the Clyde.

Ben Lomond is only one of the mountains on the skyline, which include peaks in the Trossachs and around Crianlarich, more than 30 miles (48km) away. A glimpse of the university tower 11½ miles (18½km) to the east, is a reminder that the city of Glasgow lies upriver. And on the

eastern edge of Dumbarton itself the much-quarried Dumbuck Hill was once another of the neighbourhood volcanoes.

On high ground to the north of the town, Overtoun Estate, based on an ornate Scottish baronial mansion house completed in 1862 and with biblical texts carved around its elegant entrance, is now a public park, with a nature trail through woodlands and deep in a shady glen.

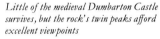

Little of the medieval Dumbarton Castle survives, but the rock's twin peaks afford excellent viewpoints

West of the Leven, in the angle it makes with the Clyde, Levengrove Park is laid out with lawns and gardens. Within it is the site of the old manor house of Cardross, where the ailing King Robert the Bruce spent the last few years of his life until his death in 1329, entertaining guests, enjoying falconry and encouraging the building of ships, which in later years became Dumbarton's principal industry.

Shipbuilding has died out here now, as the view from the castle down over the levelled sites of the old shipyards makes clear. But the Ship Model Experiment Tank used by Denny's of Dumbarton has been restored as a museum. In its long indoor channel, artificial waves could be created to test the stability of scale-model ships in different sea conditions.

The museum also recalls the curious Denny-Mumford helicopter, a pioneering design of before the First World War.

In Millport, Great Cumbrae, a natural phenomenon and a few touches of paint combine to produce Crocodile Rock

*A short climb up Duncryne Hill just
outside Gartocharn culminates in a lovely
view over the island-studded southern
waters of Loch Lomond to the mountain
peaks in the distance*

DUNLOP

99 NS 4049
Pleasantly situated in the quiet north
Ayrshire countryside, where hedge-
lined fields dip down to little burns,
this long-settled village gave its
name to two famous products.
Dunlop cheese, first churned here in
the late 17th century, was the first
whole-milk cheese ever produced in
Scotland. A hundred years later,
local farmers bred the high-yielding
Dunlop dairy cattle, only to have
them re-christened Ayrshires.

At the far end of the old-
fashioned Main Street, Dunlop Kirk
has a fine outlook over a little valley.
Although the present building dates
from 1835, it retains several features
from a predecessor of the 1640s,
which itself stood on the site of a
church several hundred years older
again. It has many historic
memorials and notable stained-glass
windows.

EAGLESHAM

99 NS 5751
Modern building has never been
allowed to interfere with the
original layout of this conservation
village, planned in 1796 by the 10th
Earl of Eglinton. Montgomerie
Street and Polnoon Street climb a
long hillside, meeting at the top and
being linked partway up by the
shorter Mid Road, which acts as the
cross-stroke of a letter A.

Neatly restored houses face one
another across the narrowing
parkland in the centre of the A,
known as the Orry. The burn that
runs through it once powered a busy
cotton mill. But the mill burned
down at unfortunately regular
intervals and was abandoned in
1876. Only a few grass-covered
fragments of the building remain.

The name of the village should be
pronounced 'Eagles-ham'. It comes
from the Gaelic word *eaglais*,
meaning church; but the parish
church has a gilded eagle for a
weathervane, just to confuse
visitors.

EAST KILBRIDE

100 NS 6354
In 1947 this previously quiet little
village started to expand mightily as
one of Scotland's New Towns.
Some older houses originally out in
the country are now well inside the
built-up area. One is the Hunter
House Museum, boyhood home of
Dr William Hunter—whose 18th-
century collection formed the basis
of the Hunterian Museum and Art
Gallery at Glasgow University (see
page 54)—and his brother John, a
founding father of modern surgery.

On the edge of the town,
Calderglen Country Park spreads
along three miles of the valley of the
Rotten Calder River—which is far
more beautiful than its unfortunate
name. Calderglen has a mansion-
house visitor centre; nature trails
explore woodland and riverside,
rocky gorges and waterfalls; and
there are picnic lawns, gardens and a
children's zoo.

FALKIRK

100 NS 8880
A curiosity of Falkirk's busy town
centre is Tolbooth Street, at less
than 60ft (18m) from end to end the
shortest street in Britain. In Orchard
Street, a small local museum

*Little changed in appearance since the
18th century, Eaglesham village overlooks
an expanse of parkland*

includes displays of 19th-century
Dunmore pottery, which features
cheery-looking animals.

On the edges of the town,
Callendar Park has lawns, woodland
and a boating pond; Bantaskine
Park rises to a ridge top where the
Jacobite army scored a victory in
January 1746.

A well-preserved stretch of the
Romans' ditch-and-banking
Antonine Wall runs parallel with
Tamfourhill Road. Further west, an
industrial wasteland only just fails to
hide the even finer Roman site
known as Rough Castle.

Falkirk should benefit from the
planned revival, for leisure use, of
the Forth and Clyde Canal. Lock 16
at Port Downie is already the scene
of several annual canal-boat events.

FENWICK

99 NS 4643
This village in the heart of the
Ayrshire farming country (the 'w' in
its name is silent) is in two main
parts. The 18th-century cottages of
Low Fenwick were built by hand-
loom weavers, while High Fenwick
was famous for its shoemakers.
Local historians insist that the
Fenwick Weavers Society founded
in 1769 was the very first Co-
operative.

The Fulton Memorial Hall
commemorates John Fulton, a High
Fenwick shoemaker who from 1823
spent 10 years of his spare time in
constructing a beautifully detailed
orrery, which shows the movement
of the solar system, and which is
now in the main hall of the Art
Gallery and Museum in
Kelvingrove Park, Glasgow.

Fenwick's parish church of 1643

was completely rebuilt after being gutted by fire in 1929. Many original features were rescued, such as the hour-glass beside the pulpit, still turned every Sunday as the minister starts his sermon. The sand takes 40 minutes to run through, and nowadays one turn is usually enough!

This is historic Covenanter country, and in the churchyard are the marked graves of the Fenwick Martyrs, killed in the days when Government troops hunted down men and women who refused to give up worshipping in Presbyterian style. Inside the church there is the faded banner carried by the local contingent of Covenanters at battles like Drumclog and Bothwell Bridge.

FINLAYSTONE

98 NS 3673
Spreading up a hillside above the main road east of Port Glasgow, this beautiful private estate is open to visitors all through the year. Woodland walks spread out from a glen whose burn tumbles past banks of azaleas and rhododendrons, and there are picnic areas in wild-flowery clearings among the trees.

Small outhouse exhibitions feature wildlife and Scotland's Celtic heritage—in the formal gardens which are also open to the public there is a 40ft (12m) diameter pavement based on designs from the ancient Book of Kells.

Finlaystone House, which has a display of dolls and Victoriana, is open only on Sunday afternoons in summer. One of its 18th-century lairds was the 14th Earl of Glencairn, Robert Burns's first patron.

FINTRY

100 NS 6186
Deep in a glaciated valley scooped out between the green and rumpled slopes of the Fintry Hills and the Campsie Fells, this was once a cotton-milling village. But the mill closed in the 1840s and has now been restored as a private house.

Fintry is an attractively strung-out village, with many renovated

cottages dating from the cotton-mill days. The grounds of Culcreuch Castle, now a hotel, are no longer a country park, although footpaths on the estate are still open—for instance, along the side of the Endrick Water and the old mill lade (the channel carrying the water to the mill wheel); walkers should check with the hotel about access.

East of the village, a 200-yard (183m) grassy footpath from the Carron Valley road leads to the completely unexpected sight of a 90ft (27½m) waterfall called the Loup (or Leap) of Fintry, where the Endrick dashes off wide rocky ledges.

GARTOCHARN

99 NS 4286
Just behind this main-road village among the farmlands on the south-east side of Loch Lomond, a footpath to the 142ft (43m) summit of Duncryne Hill opens up a magnificent panoramic view of the loch, the lovely wooded islands at its widest southern part and the 3,000ft (914m) peaks which crowd its northern narrows.

Off the main road, Ross Loan leads towards the mainland part of the Loch Lomond nature reserve, and to the lochside mansion of Ross Priory, owned by the University of Strathclyde, whose colourful gardens are open to visitors on one Sunday in May.

Fenwick's restored parish church holds memories of turbulent times during the 17th century for the many fervent Covenanters of this region. A gravestone (left) pays tribute to one of the Fenwick Martyrs, prepared to die for their Presbyterian beliefs

The elegance of Greenbank Garden is enhanced by the lovely 18th-century mansion in its grounds. Although the house is not open to the public, the garden offers plenty to enjoy

View over Gourock and the Firth

GOUROCK

98 NS 2477
A familiar West of Scotland reference to this Clyde Coast town is to say of something at a slant that it is 'all to one side, like Gourock'. This may refer to the fact that the original buildings were only on one side of Cardwell Bay.

Many travellers know Gourock simply as a place to join a ferry: to Kilcreggan, Dunoon or Hunter's Quay. But its position, just where the estuary of the River Clyde turns south to become the Firth of Clyde, gives it some outstanding views. One of the finest sights on the Firth is from the Ashton promenade as yachts sail past a backdrop of the steeply forested hills around the Holy Loch and Loch Long. This view is seen to even better effect from the top of Tower Hill. Stairways and a footpath lead up through banks of gorse to a folly tower on the summit.

Just south of Gourock, the Cloch lighthouse was built in the 1790s and is one of the few in Britain whose entrance is off the pavement of an A-class road. In wartime, a 'boom' stretched from the Cloch to the far shore of the Firth was a defence against enemy submarines.

One curiosity about Gourock is that references to a once very profitable local product have been made in thousands of detective stories: in 1688 a Gourock fish-curer invented the red herring.

GREENBANK GARDEN

99 NS 5656
On the edge of a built-up area, this National Trust for Scotland property is a reminder of more spacious times, in the grounds of an elegant Georgian mansion which is not itself open to visitors. Behind the house, a walled garden features hedged-off areas for flowers and shrubs, fruit and vegetables.

Flowerbeds raised higher than usual allow disabled enthusiasts to help at Greenbank and to join its popular gardening courses.

GREENOCK

98 NS 2776
Although several of its traditional industries have fallen on very hard times, this town on the south bank of the Clyde is in the throes of a major redevelopment programme, part of it based on the historic Custom House Quay, from which generations of Scottish emigrants sailed to a new life overseas.

The Custom House itself is a superb listed building of 1819, with a classical façade facing the river. Greenock is very well endowed with handsome Georgian and Victorian architecture.

During the Second World War this was the assembly point for Atlantic convoys. A Cross of Lorraine, beside the magnificent viewpoint on Lyle Hill over sea lochs and faraway mountains, is the Free French memorial.

Many notable people have been natives of the town, from the 17th-century pirate, Captain Kidd, to the steam-engine pioneer, James Watt. These are featured in a display in the McLean Museum and Art Gallery, which also recalls its shipbuilding history.

In 1812, however, the Greenock yards were beaten to the honour of building the world's first seagoing steamship by the neighbouring town of Port Glasgow. A life-size modern replica of the little *Comet* is on outdoor display there.

Port Glasgow's most remarkable survival, though, is half-hidden beside one of the few remaining shipyards. The 15th- and 16th-century Newark Castle, open to the public, has fine Renaissance touches and what seems like a three-dimensional maze of inner stairways to apartments overlooking the River Clyde.

Below: extraordinary Victorian mausoleum built by the 10th Duke of Hamilton—nicknamed 'Il Magnifico'—as an appropriately extravagant setting to house his own remains

HAMILTON

100 NS7255
This substantial county town can trace its history back to the 6th century and the time of the Kingdom of Strathclyde; but it appears in early records as Cadzow and took its present name, from the wealthy landowning family who eventually became the Dukes of Hamilton, only in 1445.

Hamilton District Museum is in the oldest surviving public building in the town, originally the Hamilton Arms Inn of 1696 which was the stopping-point for the Glasgow–London coaches. Its exhibition areas include the stately 18th-century Assembly Room which retains fine ornamental plasterwork and a musicians' gallery.

There is a collection of horse-drawn vehicles, from a fire-engine to a hearse, as well as vintage cars and a gleaming array of horse-brasses.

Next door to the District Museum is a building of 1842 which started life as the Duke of Hamilton's indoor riding school, but is now the museum of a famous regiment, the Cameronians (Scottish Rifles). Raised in a single day in 1689, the regiment has served in all the major wars.

The extensive museum collection includes medals, badges, weapons, prints and photographs silverware and the massive silver-bound Key of the Khyber Pass, which was actually a regimental sports trophy!

The Cameronians were disbanded in 1968, but not before, as the museum shows, they had gained a remarkable number of Victoria Crosses and provided an unusually high number of generals.

Near these two museums, on the edge of Strathclyde Country Park (see page 89), stands Hamilton's most remarkable building—the mausoleum built for himself by Alexander, the 10th Duke of Hamilton. It seems rather out of the way, but only because Hamilton Palace, which was close by, was demolished in 1927.

Alexander was a man of great wealth and a certain eccentricity, who acquired from his similarly inclined father-in-law an ornate Ancient Egyptian sarcophagus in which he decided he would be buried. To contain it, he

Transport is the theme in this part of the Hamilton District Museum

commissioned the mausoleum, which was finished in the 1850s, complete with burial vaults deep in the earth below, a splendid mosaic marble floor and a soaring dome. The mausoleum shows its back view to the approach road; from the lawns to the north the main entrance is seen to have twin staircases guarded by abysmally badly carved lions.

Guided tours of the mausoleum show that it is a no-expense-spared memorial to a man whom even his wealthy aristocratic contemporaries called 'Il Magnifico'. It also has the longest measurable echo of any building in Europe.

Glasgow Vennel, where Robert Burns lived during his years in Irvine, now boasts a Burns heritage centre

HELENSBURGH

98NS2982

This pleasant residential town and sailing resort on the Firth of Clyde was founded in the 18th century by Sir James Colquhoun of Luss, who gallantly named it after his wife. Its finest building is Hill House, a National Trust for Scotland property completed in 1904 to a design by Charles Rennie Mackintosh.

Helensburgh's most famous son was television pioneer John Logie Baird, who was born here in 1888; and Henry Bell was serving as Provost of the town in 1812 when his *Comet*, the world's first seagoing steamship, was launched at Port Glasgow (see page 80).

To the east, Ardmore peninsula has a nature trail round curving bays which attract crowds of waders and wildfowl. Much larger, the Rosneath peninsula across the Gareloch has a string of little towns and villages along its coast; a magnificent outlook from near the television mast above Kilcreggan; and a very peaceful resting place at the hillside Barbour Cemetery on the west side, where there are topiary-worked hedges, great sweeps of trimmed rhododendron bankings and a fine view through a screen of trees to Loch Long.

IRVINE

98NS3239

Although it has modern industrial estates on its outskirts, this is at heart a historic Ayrshire town with a very strong Robert Burns connection. He came here to learn the flax-dressing trade which might have augmented the meagre income from his farm. His house in the Glasgow Vennel, and the heckling shed where he worked, have been restored as a Burns heritage centre.

He made many friends in the town. In 1826, many years after his death, two of them were founder members of the Irvine Burns Club, which has the longest uninterrupted history of all the hundreds of Burns

Plaque on the cottage where Burns stayed while learning flax-dressing

Clubs throughout the world. Its collection of Burns manuscripts, letters, first editions and memorabilia is probably the finest in existence.

Irvine's massive Magnum Centre has indoor sports facilities and a theatre. Adjoining it, 150 acres of industrial wasteland have been landscaped into a Beach Park, with nature trails, picnic areas, a boating pond and a Sea World exhibition.

Shipbuilding at Irvine petered out in 1937, but an old riverside quay has been restored as the Scottish Maritime Museum. Open days show off its fine collection of smaller seagoing and estuary vessels like coasters, tugs and puffers.

The Garnock, a tug built in 1956 and, following damage in 1984, now in the Scottish Maritime Museum of Irvine Harbour, which is largely turned over to a leisure and resource centre

IRVINE VALLEY

99NS5637

This is the middle valley of the River Irvine, where the little textile towns of Newmilns and Darvel spread along the waterside, while farms and woodlands climb to open moorland high above.

Just west of Darvel, an imposing roadside memorial to Alexander Morton recalls that, in 1867, he set

up the first power-loom in the valley and revolutionised its lace-making from a cottage employment to something with a worldwide export trade.

Although it has gone through some hard times, the industry has updated itself by adding Terylene production to the traditional and more expensive lace. Fourteen companies still employ around 1,000 workers. Their curtains and tablecloths are in local shops and showrooms; but there is little demand in the valley itself for one profitable line—Terylene yashmaks for the Middle East.

Away from textiles, there is a memorial in the middle of Darvel to a boy who was brought up on one of the bleak hill farms, was educated at a tiny moorland school, went to London, and became world-famous as Sir Alexander Fleming, a Nobel Prizewinner for his work in the discovery of penicillin.

KILBARCHAN

99 NS 4063

Towards the end of the 17th century, this was one of the villages which turned from agriculture to hand-loom weaving, a trade which survived until as late as the 1950s. A house in the Barngreen became first of all a private museum, and then a National Trust for Scotland property called the Weaver's Cottage.

As an original carved lintel shows, it was built in 1723 for the Bryden family of weavers, and a loom was worked here until the 1940s. The cottage is very well stocked, not simply with a restored and working hand-loom, but also with the furniture and furnishings of generations long since gone, kitchen equipment, and tools of the weaver's trade. It has displays on the history of the village and an explanation of how Kilbarchan exported tartans, shawls, and even ponchos for South America.

KILLEARN

99 NS 5286

People who pass quickly through usually fail to notice that this attractive residential village, situated high up as it is, has a fine view west towards Loch Lomond. Killearn is keen on its history: for instance, a modern sign outside the restored toll cottage shows the charges in 1841 for berlins, diligences, curricles and wains.

Prominent in the centre of Killearn is a tall monument to the 16th-century scholar George Buchanan, a tutor in the household of Mary Queen of Scots. After her downfall, he published a vicious attack on her in his *Detection*, a book in which a later historian claimed to have detected 'ten categorical lies in 125 words'.

South of Killearn, Glengoyne distillery has produced malt whisky for more than 150 years. A reception centre is the starting-point for guided tours of the distillery, behind

This replica of a 15th-century suit of armour was made for Lord Howard de Walden; it forms part of his fine collection of arms and armour in the beautifully restored Dean Castle

which the burn which provides its all-important clear-water supply tumbles over a fall down a wooded glen.

KILMARNOCK

99 NS 4237

Although he never lived here, Kilmarnock has a very strong Robert Burns connection. In 1786 the local printer John Wilson published his first collection of poems, and copies of that 'Kilmarnock edition' now change hands for thousands of pounds. In the Burns Precinct, part of the town-centre shopping area, a plaque marks the site of Wilson's printing shop, and an ornate red-sandstone Burns Monument in balustraded and battlemented baronial style, stands at the highest level of Kay Park.

Other places popular with visitors are the art gallery and museum in the Dick Institute, and the Johnnie Walker whisky distillery, founded in 1820 and one of the busiest in the world.

On the northern outskirts of the town, riverside and woodland walks thread their way through Dean Castle Country Park. The castle itself is a beautifully restored building based on a 14th-century keep. Guided tours show off rooms, from banqueting hall to a dungeon; and there are three internationally famous collections: of tapestries, arms and armour, and historic musical instruments.

Dean Castle Country Park visitor enjoys a ride on a contemplative old lion

KILSYTH

100 NS 7178

Soldiers who fought in the Civil War Battle of Kilsyth would not recognise the 1645 battlefield now. It lies under a reservoir for the Forth and Clyde Canal, on the edge of the public park around Colzium House, which has a local museum and a fine little theatre.

Kilsyth's weaving, coal-mining and quarrying have all gone. But the old quarry at Auchinstarry has been imaginatively turned into a picnic, boating and rock-climbing practice area.

South-east of Kilsyth, Craigmarloch was where canal boats used to pause at the far end of their cruises from Glasgow. The tea room and putting green provided for passengers have disappeared, but the old stables may be rebuilt as a visitor centre.

Cruising on the Forth and Clyde Canal

KIRKINTILLOCH

100 NS6573
Although it is well inland, and not even on a major river, from 1782 to 1945 Kirkintilloch was a shipbuilding town, thanks to its position on the Forth and Clyde Canal. Its yards built not only canal boats, but also dozens of tugs and small-capacity freighters for the west coast of Scotland, England and Wales, Russia, Egypt, India, Chile and Brazil.

Down from Southbank Road, a pneumatic hammer rescued from a demolished iron foundry marks the site of Hay's Yard, which survived on repair work until 1961. The modern building here is a boat-house for the Seagull Trust, which runs canal cruises for the disabled.

Two museums stand close together near the Cross. The Barony Chambers features displays on the town's industrial and household life in years gone by, while the Auld Kirk—originally St Mary's Parish Church of 1644—has changing exhibitions, art and photographic shows.

West of Kirkintilloch, the Georgian stables by the canal at Glasgow Road Bridge have been restored as a restaurant. This is also the base for several cruise boats which sail along the wooded and winding stretch of the canal to Cadder (see page 73); there are restaurant cruises as well as meals on dry land.

LANARK

101 NS8843
This settled county town has a long and dramatic history. William Wallace lived here before starting his campaign, in the last few years of the 13th century, against the occupying English army of Edward I. In 1666, thousands of Covenanters gathered to defy the religious demands of Charles II.

More peacefully, the old tradition of checking the burgh boundaries continues as part of the Lanimer Week celebrations in June, which end with the enthusiastic crowning of the Lanimer Queen.

Lanark's livestock market brings in farmers from miles round, but crowds are no longer attracted to the racecourse on Lanark Moor. It was taken out of the regular 'circuit' in 1977, although the Lanark Silver Bell is the oldest horse-racing trophy in Scotland. Today, the racecourse is used for much smaller meetings and events like harness racing.

Most of the Moor has been turned into a country park with open spaces, woodlands and a boating loch, and there is a fine golf course.

LARGS

98 NS2058
Partly a holiday resort, and a favourite place for retirement, Largs has good facilities for water sports, bowling and golf, and looks across the Firth of Clyde to Cumbrae (see page 76).

It is well provided with parks and gardens. The largest of these is Douglas Park, which rises to a splendid viewpoint 650ft (198m) above sea-level, overlooking the Firth, its major islands, the long peninsula of Kintyre and the faraway peaks of Jura.

A small museum off Main Street has displays on the history of the town. Behind it, almost all that remains of the old parish church is the elaborate burial aisle of the Montgomeries of Skelmorlie, which retains its faded but beautifully painted 17th-century wooden ceiling.

The Battle of Largs in 1263 resulted in the Scottish victory which led the Vikings to abandon their control over the Western Isles. Every autumn, the Norsemen come back to Largs, but only for a Viking Festival of music, dancing, theatre, parades, sports events and bonfires.

Near the marina south of the town known as Largs Yacht Haven, Kelburn Country Centre has very attractive walks around the wooded ravine of the Kel Burn, with a silver-

Lanark—peaceful town with a history

The Pencil, Largs, commemorates 1263

threaded waterfall cascading into a dark sandstone pool. There are fine specimen trees such as cedars and redwoods, 1,000-year-old yews and a freak weeping larch.

The 18th-century farm buildings called the South Offices have been converted into a visitor centre. Children have an adventure playground nearby, while adults can try the assault course built by the Commandos for their own training.

Kelburn Castle, home of the Earl of Glasgow, dates in part from the 12th century, and may be the oldest still-inhabited house in Scotland.

LOCHWINNOCH

98NS3558
There is no point in searching the map for a stretch of water with this name, because it has been known for

hundreds of years now as Castle Semple Loch (see page 74).

Set back from its banks, the village of Lochwinnoch has a mostly 19th-century High Street with brightly painted houses. Lochwinnoch Community Museum does not concern itself with affairs outside the parish. Instead, it puts on changing displays about the history of village industries such as spinning and weaving, furniture-making and coopering, and about the domestic concerns, dress and recreations of generations past.

The Aird Meadows, once drained of water but now gradually filling again, are the site of an excellent RSPB visitor centre. From a first-floor viewing gallery, and from ground-level hides, visitors can unobtrusively watch great crested grebes, moorhen, mallard and dozens of other species of ducks and wildfowl, as well as birds of the reedland and the woodland fringe.

MILNGAVIE

99NS5574
If there was any sense to it, the spelling of the name of this attractive residential town north of Glasgow would be something like Mill-guy, to match its pronunciation.

Milngavie Railway Station is the start of the 95-mile (153km) West Highland Way. In its early stages, walkers take a footpath alongside the Allander Water, cross the open spaces of Drumclog Moor and then go past the once-coppiced oaks and birches of Mugdock Wood, on their way—eventually—to Fort William.

Above the town are situated the twin Victorian reservoirs of

Mugdock and Craigmaddie, banked by heathery slopes and stands of Scots pine. Here the water supply which comes through a 26-mile (40km) tunnel from Loch Katrine finally reaches the surface again. The reservoir grounds are a popular strolling area.

Yet another major public open space is Mugdock Country Park, with two ruined castles—Mugdock and Craigend—in its grounds. It also has a hilltop folly tower, built about 1810 for no reason other than to improve the view, a sycamore avenue, and a quiet little loch.

MOTHERWELL

100NS7557
In the middle of the 19th century, Motherwell expanded hugely from a modest village into a sprawling iron- and steelworks town.

Remarkably, the Dalzell estate—pronounced simply 'Dee ell'—has survived virtually unscathed. This is a magnificent stretch of woodland dipping down towards the Clyde, landscaped at great expense as a fit setting for a massive mansion house recently restored and converted into flats. There are drives and pathways past ornamental bridges, terraces, grottoes, a miniature classical temple and a Japanese garden.

On the low ground of Dalzell, right on the banks of the Clyde, Barons Haugh is an RSPB reserve where grebes, mallard, teal and tufted duck are seen in summer, and whooper swans spend the winter months.

Milngavie town centre

NEW LANARK and THE FALLS OF CLYDE

101 NS8844

The village of New Lanark and the Falls of Clyde nature reserve are complementary to each other: the tremendous water power of the only series of major cascades on the River Clyde was what led to the building of the village in this precise location, on steep wooded banks below the old county town of Lanark.

In the 18th century, poets, artists and enthusiasts for 'romantic' landscapes began to write breathless prose and verse, and paint generally exaggerated pictures, featuring the zigzag rock-walled gorge where the Clyde in spate crashed over the falls of Bonnington Linn, Corra Linn and Dundaff Linn.

But industrialists had their eyes on the place too. David Dale, one of Scotland's greatest cotton magnates, realised that the force of the falls could be harnessed to drive the newly invented cotton spinning machinery. However, the Falls of Clyde were remote in those days, and houses as well as factory-style mills would have to be built if a workforce of any size was to be assembled.

Falls of Clyde (left), the power that gave rise to the once-thriving mills of New Lanark (below)

Dale's first mill started spinning in 1786. The business boomed, the village expanded year by year—and New Lanark as it stands today, its original *raison d'être* a thing of the past, is a living and lived-in museum of a great industry and of a succession of enlightened employers whose control of almost all aspects of their workers' lives would nevertheless not be tolerated today.

David Dale and later his son-in-law Robert Owen were involved in the running of the mills and the village until Owen left—unhappy with changes to the system insisted on by his partners—in 1824. The company provided not only good-quality housing and dormitory accommodation for the orphan children who made up part of the workforce, but also a co-operative shop, a savings bank, a crèche, an excellent school and the grandly titled New Institution for the Formation of Character. All the major original buildings remain, with that almost careless elegance of so much Georgian design.

Although the work was hard and the hours were long, Owen in particular was a world pioneer in education, putting into action in this tucked-away Lanarkshire mill village what had previously been only well-intentioned theories. Adults, of course, were not forgotten, and Caithness Row in the village is a reminder that dispossessed smallholders from the northern counties came to settle in New Lanark instead of taking the more familiar emigrant route to North America.

As generations passed, ownership of the village changed and the work was diversified—latterly, canvas, tents, fishing-nets and ropes were produced as well as cotton. Then an inevitable run-down began, and in 1968 the last mill fell silent. New Lanark, a village famous in social and industrial textbooks all over the world, was in the utmost danger of being demolished. But it staged a remarkable fight-back.

Public and private organisations rallied round. For the first time since the village was built, some houses were sold off to owners who guaranteed to make careful renovations. Local authority and central government money, manpower, expertise and support were all provided. A conservation trust was formed, small businesses started up, more houses were renovated for renting to incoming tenants, and in 1983 the local district council finally made a compulsory purchase of the tall, many-windowed mill buildings which by that time

were in the possession of a scrap-metal company.

The massive restoration programme continues. Visitors in their tens of thousands arrive every year; footpaths and a heritage trail show off the historic buildings; special events like Victorian-costume fairs crowd the streets. And yet New Lanark is no half-bogus exhibition area; after more than 200 years it is a living village still.

A fair head of water comes pounding down from the gorge which opens up only slightly at the village. But the Falls of Clyde have been harnessed to an extent that even David Dale would never have dreamed of. An unobtrusive hydro-electric power-station drains off most of the water before it tumbles over Bonnington Linn and Corra Linn, but pipes it back into the river before the final bend towards the village.

The restored New Lanark dyeworks is a visitor centre run by the Scottish Wildlife Trust. Its two-mile nature reserve takes in the whole of the thickly wooded gorge and all three of the falls. Both the centre and the network of nature trails beyond it show off the geology of the gorge; the various wild flowers, ferns and mosses which colonise its damp and shadowy inner reaches; the wildlife of its oak and ash, birch, pine and hazel

Potter's workshop, one of the many small enterprises that have taken advantage of New Lanark's recent revival as a lived-in museum

woodlands; herons, dippers, wagtails and the kingfishers which dart around the gorge in flashes of brilliant blue.

There is more than wildlife interest in the gorge, though. The 15th-century Corra Castle is a dizzily-sited ruin high on the far bank. Above the power-station stands the 'hall of mirrors' built in 1798 to give unsuspecting visitors to it the impression that they were walking right into some kind of indoor waterfall.

And, on the flat-topped 'island' at Bonnington Linn, there used to be a moss-lined picnic house—for visitors who enjoyed damp and spray and crashing water all around.

Even without that full, natural flow of water, the gorge remains an imposing place, although one easily seen from the pleasant woodland pathways high up on both sides. But on four pre-advertised days every year the power-station tunnels are closed. The Clyde comes thundering down the full width of the channel it is generally denied, and the majestic roaring river which so affected Wordsworth, Coleridge, Scott and Turner is there once more for everyone to see.

PAISLEY

99 NS 4864

Although the town and the city merge unobtrusively into each other, visitors to Paisley should be in no doubt that it is a place entirely independent of Glasgow. At the heart of the modern town is Paisley Abbey, originally a 12th-century building enlarged from an earlier priory, but burned down in 1307 by Edward I's troops because the abbots and monks were firmly on the home side during the Independence Wars.

The abbey's complete rebuilding, and the careful renovation work which continues to the present day, are due partly to the fact that it was connected with the Breton French FitzAlan family, who were given a 12th-century grant of vast areas of land in the west of Scotland.

Walter FitzAlan was made High Steward of Scotland. His descendants took Stewart as their surname. And after Walter Stewart married Robert the Bruce's sister, their son became Robert II of Scotland, the first of a long line of Stewart—later, Stuart—kings and queens.

Prince Charles is a modern link with the earliest days of Paisley and its abbey. He is 27th in direct line of descent from Walter FitzAlan and, among his other titles, the High Steward of Scotland today.

In amongst all its historic monuments, fine wood-carvings, stonework and stained-glass windows, Paisley Abbey is still a busy parish church today, and it has a very strong musical tradition.

The social and industrial history of the town is one of the themes of displays in Paisley Museum and Art Gallery.

Until only a few generations ago,

Telescope at Coats Observatory, one of the best-equipped observatories in the country, with displays on space flight, astronomy and meteorology

Paisley was mainly a textile town. For about 100 years till the 1870s it exported one famous product all over the fashionable world: the beautiful silk-woven Paisley-pattern shawl, made originally to Kashmiri designs. More than 700 shawls are on show in a special museum gallery.

Elsewhere in the town, the Sma' Shot Cottages Museum occupies a restored Victorian house which also contains a re-created 18th-century hand-loom weaver's workshop. The 'small shot' was a binding thread the weavers used, and Sma' Shot Day was their traditional holiday.

The Coats family, whose world-wide cotton thread business started in Paisley, were great benefactors to the town. In 1880 Thomas Coats put up the money for an astronomical telescope to start an observatory in the area. The Coats Observatory now makes weather-satellite and

seismic observations, as well as having displays on astronomy, meteorology and space flight, and a planetarium open to visitors.

Immediately to the south of Paisley, the Gleniffer Braes Country Park rises to 1,000 acres of high-level moorland, with picnic areas and a nature trail, and a fine elevated view over the town and the whole of the Glasgow basin.

The steep climb up the Braes was a test route used by the Arrol-Johnston company which built cars in Paisley before the First World War. In the 1920s, the Beardmore factory concentrated on taxis, and thousands of the traditional 'London cabs' were Paisley products.

In the heart of Paisley, the 19th-century neo-classical town hall is situated by the White Cart Water

Queen Victoria watches over Paisley town centre

STRATHAVEN

100 NS 7044

Actually pronounced Stray-ven, this is one of those slightly off-the-main-tourist-track places, which deserves far more visitors than usually come its way. It is a compact town, with fine public parks beside the little Powmillon Burn which, lower down, runs past grassy banks once reserved for the drying of hand-woven linen.

A heritage trail includes such

Tiptoe through the tulips at Rouken Glen (left), or spot a swallowtail at the Butterfly Kingdom (right)

it is centred on a 200-acre man-made loch used for dinghy sailing, canoeing, sailboarding, water-skiing and rowing—it was the venue for the Commonwealth Games rowing events in 1986.

Hamilton Racecourse is on the edge of the park, which also has two separate golf courses and a golf driving range, football pitches, tennis courts and bowling greens, caravan and camping sites, a fairground and an ice rink.

The visitor centre has displays on

Strathclyde Country Park (left) is a mecca for sports enthusiasts—both the land-based and the watery variety

ROUKEN GLEN

99 NS 5458

Because it lies just outside the city boundaries, this one-time Glasgow public park was the subject of a recent dispute between neighbouring authorities about which of them would pay for its upkeep. In the early 1980s it lay dismally unattended for some time, but it is now under the control of Eastwood District Council.

The park has two very different landscapes. Part of it includes spreading lawns, a fine formal garden and a boating pond. But there is also a deep, wooded glen with riverside pathways and tumbling rocky waterfalls.

A garden centre at the edge of the park includes the hot-houses of Eastwood Butterfly Kingdom. Tropical butterflies such as the Blue Mountain, Great Mormon, Chinese Peacock and Common Jezebel are all bred here, as well as the more familiar Red Admiral and Swallowtail. Slightly less appealing are the scorpions and red-legged tarantulas of the Insect Kingdom.

features of the town as the hilltop ruin of Strathaven Castle, home for a time in the Civil War of a Duchess of Hamilton expelled from Hamilton Palace (see page 81) because of her hearty distaste for Cromwell.

Six black coach-horses from Flanders, brought to Strathaven Castle and crossed with local mares, began one of the strains of the famous Clydesdales.

At the John Hastie Museum there are displays on the local battles during Covenanting times, the rise and decline of the weaving industry, and the story of James Wilson, the Strathaven weaver executed for his part in the Radical Rising of 1820.

STRATHCLYDE COUNTRY PARK

100 NS 7258

Laid out on both sides of the River Clyde and of the M74, and occupying the open ground between Hamilton and Motherwell, this 1,650-acre park specialises in outdoor activities. Opened in 1978,

the natural history of the area, and maps showing that the old mining village of Bothwellhaugh, which has now completely disappeared, stood partly on the land flooded for the loch.

Every Easter, the road that rises from the watersports centre is used by racing cars competing in the opening round of the Scottish hill-climb championship.

The park is very well provided with nature trails and historical walks. One, from the site of a Roman fort and bath-house, explores the area occupied briefly in the 1820s by the model Orbiston Community, started by two disciples of Robert Owen, who put his social theories into practice at New Lanark (see page 86).

Other trails for which self-guiding leaflets are available include a woodland walk in the valley of the South Calder Water; a stroll through an old willow wood; a scrubland trail; and the Dry Bridge Trail, which follows old estate roads through plantations of oak and ash, beech, sycamore and lime, and thickets of golden broom.

Right: this impressive modern statue of Robert the Bruce stands in the rotunda commemorating the Battle of Bannockburn when, against heavy odds, Bruce's forces won a victory crucial for Scottish independence

STIRLING

100 NS 7993

For hundreds of years, the town of Stirling more or less shared the status of capital of Scotland with the city of Edinburgh, and the two places have several features in common: a heavily defended castle on top of an imposing volcanic rock, a royal palace and many fine houses originally built for wealthy courtiers.

Stirling was a royal burgh from about the year 1125, but clearly had royal connections long before that. Later, the castle was a favourite residence of the Stuart kings and queens.

James IV built many of the existing defences. In the middle of the 16th century James V, who encouraged French architects and stonemasons to work in Scotland, commissioned the Palace which stands at the heart of the fortified hilltop site. And James VI largely remodelled the Chapel Royal.

A long restoration programme is almost completed; most of the buildings, the defenceworks, the lawns and gardens are open to visitors. The castle's elevated position provides splendid views, especially west along the flat lands of the Carse of Stirling to the mountains of the Highland Line. When it is floodlit at night, the hilltop fortress looks particularly

impressive from that western approach.

There are pleasant pathways on the flanks of the hill, outside the castle's defences: along the Back Walk which follows the original town walls; and onto the lower-lying Gowan Hill where, among the brightly flowering gorse, watchers from the castle could see executions taking place.

Sir William Wallace (below) looks out from a vantage point on the Wallace Monument (left) which surmounts Abbey Craig and contains displays on many Scottish heroes besides Wallace

The National Trust for Scotland runs a fine visitor centre on the castle esplanade, with an audio-visual theatre and a well-stocked bookshop. The area of Stirling just below the castle is known as the Top of the Town. It is crowded with historic buildings, all stopping places on a Heritage Walk.

Dating from the 15th century, the Church of the Holy Rude retains its original open-timber roof. An interior wall was built across the middle of this church after a violent disagreement in 1656 split its congregation into two incompatible factions, but this was fortunately taken down 280 years later.

The Earl of Mar's mansion of the 1570s, known as Mar's Wark, survives as little more than a façade.

Argyll's Lodging is now a youth hostel. And the old grammar school was long ago turned into the Portcullis Hotel.

Behind the Church of the Holy Rude, Cowane's Hospital, now the Guildhall, was originally a 17th-century almshouse for members of the town's Merchants' Guild who had fallen on hard times. The statue of John Cowane, who endowed it, stands above the main doorway. Alongside the Guildhall, a pleasant bowling green whose turf was first laid in 1712 is one of the oldest in Scotland.

During the Independence Wars, when Edward I and II of England were trying to take control of Scotland as well, Stirling was the scene of two major battles. In 1297 William Wallace, the Guardian of Scotland, swept down from the north to defeat an English army gathered at Stirling Bridge.

So it was appropriate that the summit of Abbey Craig, another volcanic rock overlooking the site of the battle, was chosen in the 1860s as the location of a national Wallace Monument. This is a soaring Scottish Baronial tower, quarried from the rocks of Abbey Craig itself. It stands on the 310ft (94½m) hilltop, and rises another 220ft (67m) to a breezy viewing gallery from which there is a magnificent all-round outlook.

The climb to the top is a long one, up 242 steps, mostly round a spiral staircase. But there is an audio-visual theatre on the ground floor, in the room where Wallace's massive two-handed sword is on display, and there are exhibition rooms on three other levels.

The Hall of Arms has swords and muskets on the walls, and pictures of medieval Stirling. In the darkened Hall of Heroes, busts of famous Scots are spotlighted in turn as a taped commentary gives brief biographies. One level higher still, there is a room devoted to illustrations of places connected with Wallace's life and soldierly career.

Outside, Abbey Craig itself has a network of clifftop and woodland pathways, where wild flowers brighten the glades of oak and sycamore, elm and pine.

Immediately south of Stirling there is an even more famous battlefield and an even more significant historic site. The Borestone was Robert the Bruce's command post before the Battle of Bannockburn in 1314, the victory which finally re-established Scotland's independence.

A National Trust for Scotland

Heritage Centre here includes a splendid mural of the battle, an audio-visual display and a general historical exhibition. Through a screen of trees, there are lawns leading to a rotunda which acts as a memorial to the battle, with a striking modern statue of Bruce, mounted and armed, against the skyline.

Another historic site near Stirling has a much more peaceful background. Cambuskenneth is an attractive little village with bright gardens, on an almost island site on one of the River Forth's most exaggerated meanders around the town. It is linked to Stirling by a footbridge near a line of riverside birches.

Only low foundation walls trace the main outline of its medieval abbey, although a later and separate bell-tower has been restored and has a spiral staircase to a parapet walk. Queen Victoria took a keen interest in Cambuskenneth Abbey when the graves of James III and Queen Margaret of Scotland, buried here in the late 15th century, were discovered during an archaeological excavation. In 1865 they were reburied where the abbey's high altar once stood, under a memorial erected at Victoria's personal expense.

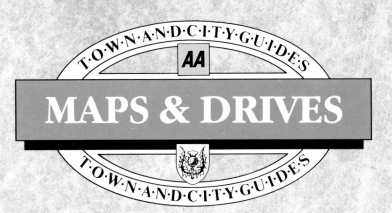

MAPS & DRIVES

Rooftop devils face a church in Helensburgh, an attractive
town on the route back to Glasgow from the lochs to the
north-west

Along the Lochs

Across the Kilpatrick Hills and down into the valley of Endrick Water, the drive continues along Loch Lomond, Loch Long and Gare Loch to the Clyde Estuary and Dumbarton.

From the centre of Glasgow follow signs Dumbarton to leave by Great Western Road A82. At Anniesland Cross turn right onto the A739 signed Drymen, Bearsden, and in 1¼ miles at the roundabout take 1st exit onto the A809, again signed Drymen. Pass through the suburb of **Bearsden** *and in ¼ mile turn right following signs for Stirling. Half a mile further at roundabout take 2nd exit. The drive ascends over the edge of the Kilpatrick Hills, passing after 5¼ miles the AA Viewpoint of Queen's View, Auchineden, on the left.*

Gradually descend to the valley of Endrick Water. One mile beyond Croftamie turn left onto the A811 signed Erskine Bridge. [At the village of **Gartocharn** *a side-road to the left leads to a short, steep footpath to the summit of Duncryne, which offers a panoramic view including Loch Lomond.]*

Three miles beyond Gartocharn at the edge of **Balloch,** *pass a road on the right for the Balloch Castle Country Park and Visitor Centre.* The 19th-century castle, contained within 200 acres of parkland beside Loch Lomond, is open to the public. Balloch is situated at the southern tip of Loch Lomond, which is 24 miles long and the largest expanse of inland water in Britain. Steamer excursions are run from Balloch Pier in the summer, and the loch's many islands make it an ideal water for such recreations as sailing, water-skiing and fishing.

A quarter of a mile past Balloch at the roundabout take 2nd exit and at the next roundabout take 2nd exit. At the following roundabout take 3rd exit signed Crianlarich onto the A82. In 1¼ miles pass the Duck Bay Picnic Area on the right. Offshore is Inchmurrin, Loch Lomond's largest island, which is believed to have been the site of St Mirren's monastery in the 6th century and contains the ruins of Lennox Castle.

Follow the shores of Loch Lomond, passing Luss and going through Inverbeg. There are views of the many wooded islets and the hills beyond the eastern shore including Ben Lomond (3,192ft/973m). A side-road to the right of the A82 leads to the picturesque, largely Victorian village of Luss itself with its shingle bay and pier on Luss Water. At Inverbeg there is a passenger ferry to Rowardennan at the foot of Ben Lomond.

At Tarbet keep forward onto the A83, signed Campbeltown, to cross the narrow neck of land that separates Loch Lomond from Loch Long, for Arrochar. Among the mountains that can be seen in this area are The Cobbler (Ben Arthur) (2,891ft/881m), Beinn Narnain (3,036ft/925m) and The Brack (2,583ft/787m).

Turn sharp left at Arrochar, signed Helensburgh, to join the A814 along the shores of Loch Long. After 7 miles pass the Finnart oil terminal and ascend to cross another neck of land separating Gare Loch from Loch Long. Pass a viewpoint and picnic site on the left before descending to the junction with the B833. [Here, by turning right onto the B833, a 19-mile diversion can be made to tour the Rosneath peninsula.] The main route bears left and shortly enters Garelochhead. Continue down the eastern side of the loch. The drive passes the MOD establishments and nuclear submarine base at Faslane.

Follow the road through Shandon and Rhu. At Rhu the gardens of Glenaran are open to the public at certain times of year.

Shortly, reach **Helensburgh**. This is an attractive residential town and popular tourist centre. Of particular interest is the Hill House (NTS) considered to be the finest work of the Victorian architect, Charles Rennie Mackintosh.

Continue on the A814, following the Clyde Estuary, through Craigendoran and Cardross to **Dumbarton**. The town's former importance as the capital of Strathclyde is emphasised by the castle perched high on a rock overlooking the entrance to the River Clyde. As the drive leaves the town it passes several world-famous whisky distilleries.

Leave by the Glasgow road and in 2 miles turn right onto the A82. One mile further at the roundabout take 1st exit for the return along dual-carriageways, through Anniesland, to the centre of Glasgow. From this roundabout an alternative route (2½ miles shorter) can be taken via Clydebank. Take 2nd exit A814 signed Bowling to pass through Bowling and Old Kilpatrick. Go under the Erskine Bridge and later pass Clydebank and Scotstoun. Half a mile beyond the **Victoria Park** *follow signs City Centre to reach the centre of Glasgow.*
(All places in **bold type** are described in the Out of City gazetteer.)

Seafront at Helensburgh, where Gare Loch and Clyde Estuary merge

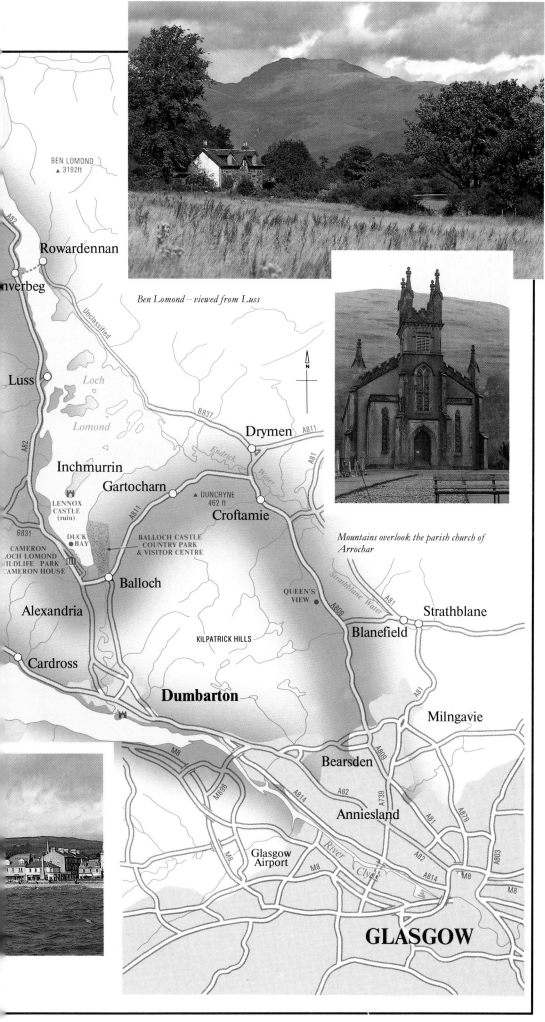

BEN LOMOND
▲ 3192ft

A82

Rowardennan

Inverbeg

Luss

Unclassified

Loch

Lomond

Ben Lomond – viewed from Luss

B837

A82

Inchmurrin

Gartocharn

LENNOX
CASTLE
(ruin)

B831

DUCK
BAY

CAMERON
LOCH LOMOND
WILDLIFE PARK
CAMERON HOUSE

Balloch

BALLOCH CASTLE
COUNTRY PARK
& VISITOR CENTRE

A811

Drymen

A811

A81

Endrick

Water

▲ DUNCRYNE
462 ft

Croftamie

N

Mountains overlook the parish church of Arrochar

Alexandria

Cardross

KILPATRICK HILLS

QUEEN'S
VIEW

Dumbarton

A909

Strathblane Water

A81

Blanefield

Strathblane

Milngavie

A81

M8

M898

A814

Bearsden

A82

A739

A909

M898

A814

Anniesland

A82

A81

A879

A803

Glasgow
Airport

M8

River

Clyde

M8

A814

M8

M8

A803

GLASGOW

95

The Trossachs

The route travels over the Campsie Fells and past the site of the Battle of Bannockburn to Stirling; then on to the Trossachs and the Queen Elizabeth Forest Park.

Take the Aberfoyle road A81 out of Glasgow. Leave the suburbs at Milngavie and continue to Strathblane. At Strathblane turn right onto the A891, signed Lennoxtown. At Lennoxtown turn left, signed Fintry, onto the B822. The road climbs out of the valley and passes the head of Campsie Glen, providing fine views to the south over Glasgow, before crossing the Campsie Fells.

After descending into the valley of the Endrick Water, turn right onto the B818, signed Denny. The road later runs alongside the Carron Valley Reservoir which is backed by attractive pine forests. Shortly beyond the dam is the **Carron Valley** Forest Car Park and Picnic Site.

One and a half miles further, at the Carron Bridge Hotel, turn left onto an unclassified road, signed Stirling. In 2 miles the road passes the small Loch Coulter Reservoir. After another 2¼ miles bear left. One mile further there are good views of the Wallace Monument and Stirling Castle.

Three-quarters of a mile after crossing the M9 turn right and then left to join the A872 at Bannockburn. Immediately to the left is the Bannockburn Battleground Heritage Centre (NTS).

In ½ mile at the roundabout take 2nd exit to reach **Stirling**. The former Royal Burgh is a focal point of Scottish history. Crowning Abbey Craig, 1 mile north-east at Causewayhead, is the 220ft-high (67m) Wallace Monument, an excellent viewpoint.

Leave Stirling by the Crianlarich road A84 and at the M9 motorway junction roundabouts take 2nd then 3rd exits. Shortly cross the River Forth and proceed along the level valley of the River Teith, passing in 3 miles on the right the road to Blair Drummond Safari Park. Two and a half miles further turn left onto the B8032, signed Deanston, then bear left, signed Callander. This road follows the course of the Teith through more undulating country.

After 6¼ miles turn right onto the B822 and shortly right again onto the A81 (no signs). In 2 miles enter Callander. This tourist centre at the confluence of the rivers Teith and Leny is overlooked to the north-west by Ben Ledi (2,873ft/876m).

Follow signs Crianlarich A84 and in 1 mile pass the hamlet of Kilmahog with its woollen mill, then turn left onto the A821 signed Aberfoyle, The Trossachs, and cross the River Leny. The road runs alongside Loch Venachar with the peak of Ben Ledi to the right. After the picturesque village of Brig o'Turk the drive enters the Queen Elizabeth Forest Park beside Loch Achray. A quarter of a mile beyond the Trossachs Hotel a 2-mile diversion can be made by keeping forward to reach the pier on the eastern end of Loch Katrine, heart of the Trossachs.

Turn left to stay on the Aberfoyle road. The drive climbs through the Achray Forest, passing after 2 miles a car park and viewpoint offering a panorama of the Trossach lochs, and ½ mile further on affords views of Loch Drunkie to the left. Beyond the 796ft (243m) summit the road descends The Duke's Pass, later offering spectacular views over the wide Forth Valley and Flanders Moss to the Campsie Fells, and passing the David Marshall Lodge Forest Park Visitor Centre and viewpoint before entering the small resort of Aberfoyle.

Leave by the Stirling road, A821, and after 1 mile branch left onto the A81, signed Callander. In ½ mile on the left is the Braeval Forest Walk and car park. Two miles further on the right is the Lake of Menteith, the only large expanse of fresh water in Scotland not called a loch. Inchmahome Priory (AM), the 13th-century ruins on one of the islands, provided a refuge for the infant Mary, Queen of Scots.

One mile further turn right onto the B8034, signed Arnprior. Later cross the River Forth and Flanders Moss and at Arnprior turn right onto the A811, then left onto an unclassifed road, signed Fintry. After 2 miles the road crosses the moors below the Fintry Hills and turns right onto the B822 (no sign) to reach **Fintry**. On the left is the road to the 14th-century Culcreuch Castle (limited opening).

Turn right onto the Killearn road B818 (no sign) then in 5½ miles join the Glasgow road, A875, and pass through **Killearn**. *Two miles further turn left onto the A81, following sign Strathblane, to Blanefield and Strathblane. At Strathblane bear right on the A81 to Glasgow.*

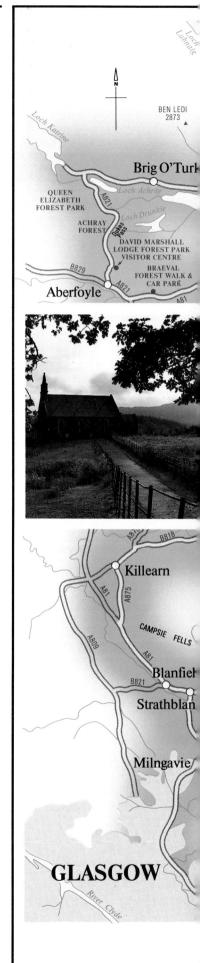

Above left: by Loch Achray on the eastern side of the Trossachs, a region where mountains, rivers, lochs and woodland create some of Scotland's loveliest countryside, the setting for Scott's Lady of the Lake

Top right: David Marshall Lodge, whose Forest Park Visitor Centre has an exhibition on Queen Elizabeth Forest Park.

An imposing presence, Stirling Castle dominates the town

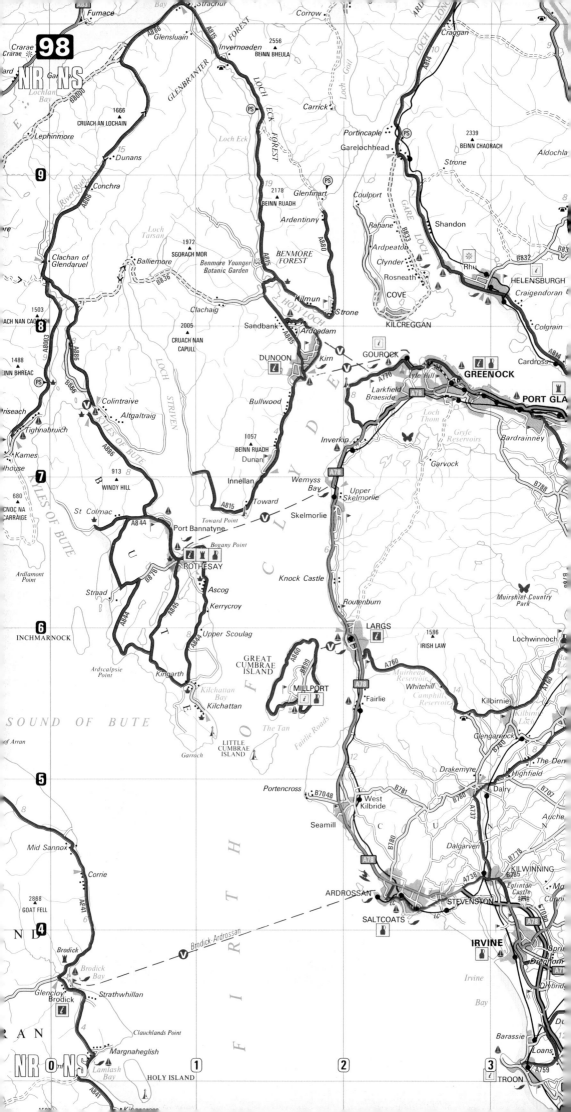

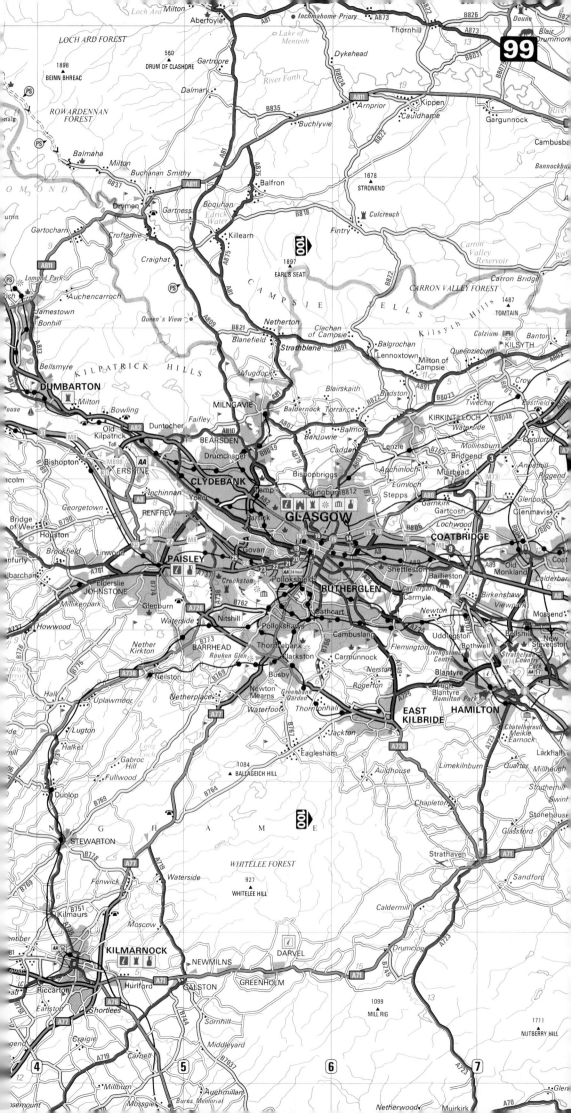

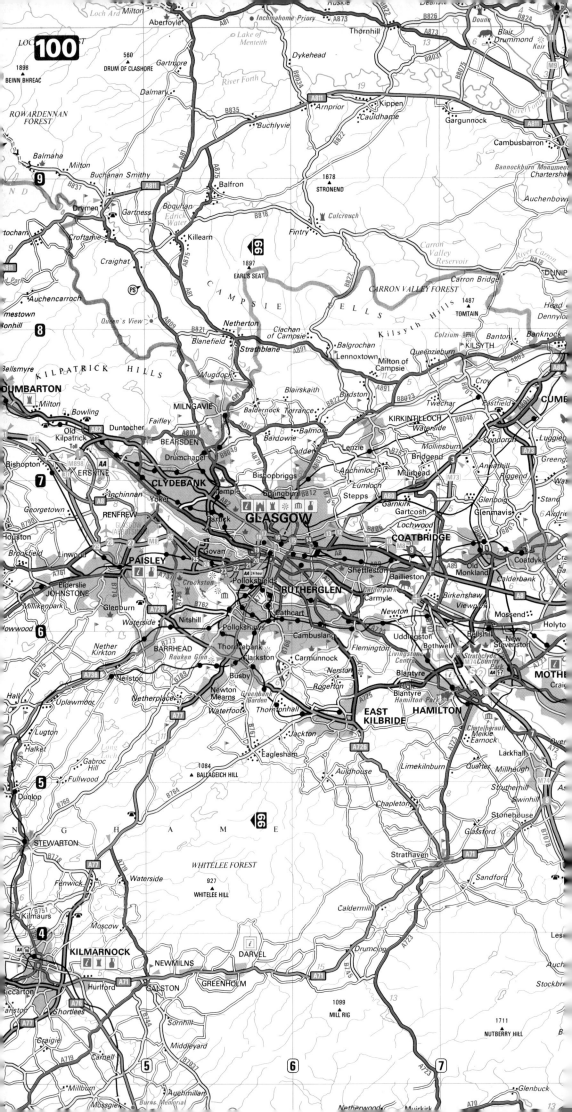

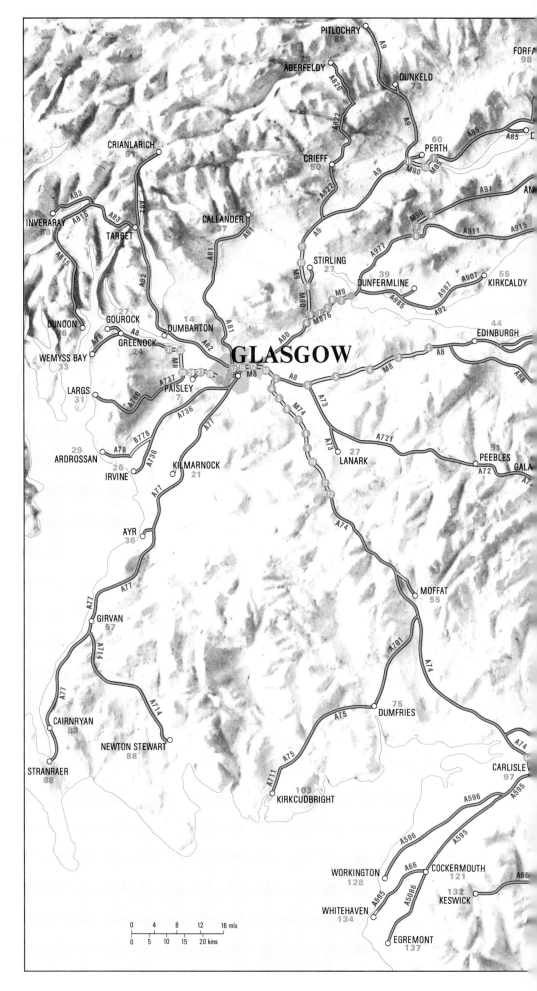

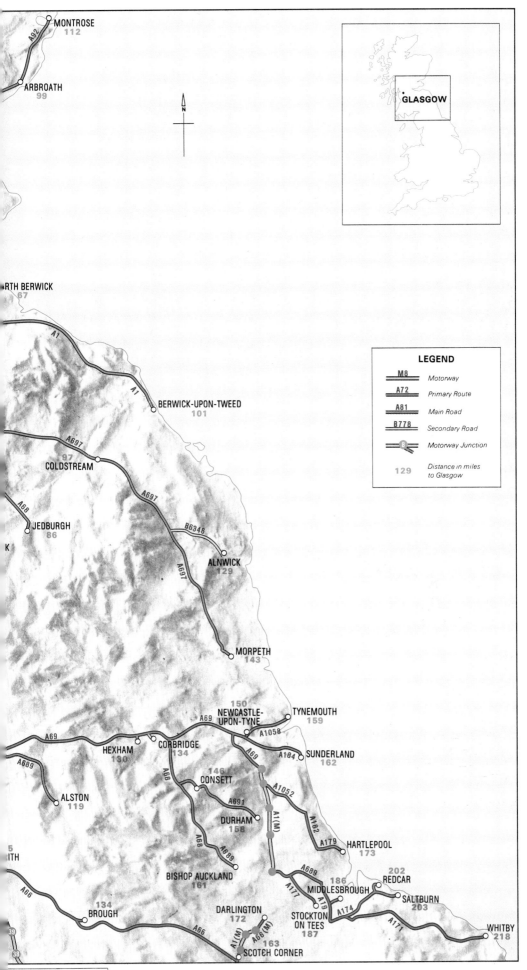

MONTROSE
112

ARBROATH
99

GLASGOW

N

RTH BERWICK
67

A1

A1

BERWICK-UPON-TWEED
101

A697

COLDSTREAM
97

A697

A68

JEDBURGH
86

B6346

A697

ALNWICK
129

A697

MORPETH
143

LEGEND

M8 — Motorway

A72 — Primary Route

A81 — Main Road

B778 — Secondary Road

8 — Motorway Junction

129 — Distance in miles to Glasgow

150
NEWCASTLE-UPON-TYNE

TYNEMOUTH
159

A69

A1058

A69 — HEXHAM 130 — CORBRIDGE 134

A69

A184 — SUNDERLAND 162

A689

A68

CONSETT
146

A1052

ALSTON
119

A691

DURHAM
158

A1(M)

A182

A179 — HARTLEPOOL 173

ITH

A68

A689

BISHOP AUCKLAND
161

A689

202
REDCAR

186
MIDDLESBROUGH

A177

A19

SALTBURN
203

A66

134
BROUGH

DARLINGTON
172

STOCKTON ON TEES
187

A174

A171

WHITBY
218

A66

A66

A1(M) — A66(M) 163

SCOTCH CORNER

39

38

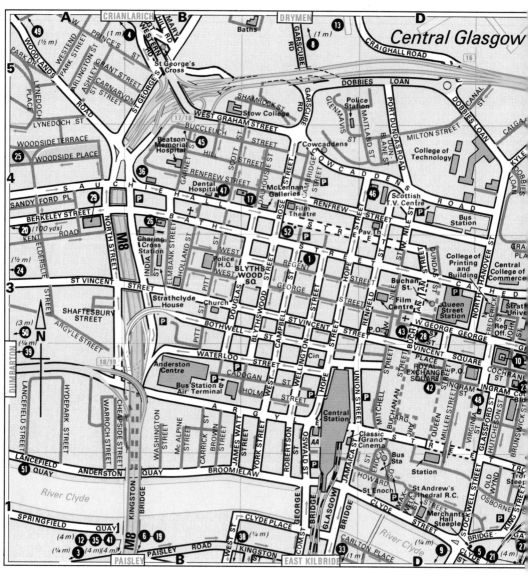

Central Glasgow

Key to Places of Interest

1 Annan Gallery	C3
2 The Barrows (The Barras)	F1
3 Bellahouston Park	A1
4 Botanic Gardens	B5
5 Briggait Centre	E1
6 Burrell Collection/Pollok Country Park	B1
7 Carmunnock	E1
8 Charles Rennie Mackintosh Centre	C5
9 Citizen's Theatre	D1
10 City Chambers	E2
11 City Hall	E2
12 Crookston Castle	A1
13 Forth and Clyde Canal	C5
14 Glasgow Cathedral	F3
15 Glasgow Cross	E1
16 Glasgow Green	E1
17 Glasgow School of Art	C4
18 Glasgow Zoo	F1

19 Haggs Castle	B1
20 Henry Wood Hall	A4
21 High Court	E1
22 Hogganfield Loch	F4
23 Hutchesons' Hall	E2
24 Kelvin Hall	A3
25 Kelvingrove	A4
26 King's Theatre	B4
27 Linn Park	E1
28 Merchant's House	D3
29 Mitchell Library	A4
30 People's Palace	F1
31 Provan Hall	F4
32 Provand's Lordship	F3
33 Queen's Park	C1
34 Robroyston	F5
35 Rosshall Park	A1
36 Royal Highland Fusiliers Museum	B4
37 Rutherglen	E1
38 Scotland Street School	C1
39 Scottish Exhibition and Conference Centre	A2
40 Springburn Museum	F4
41 602 (City of Glasgow) Squadron Museum	A1

42 Stirling's Library	D2
43 Stock Exchange	D3
44 Strathclyde University	E3
45 The Tenement House	B4
46 Theatre Royal	D4
47 Third Eye Centre	B4
48 Trades House	E2
49 University of Glasgow	A5
50 Victoria Park	A3
51 PS Waverley	A1
52 Willow Tea Rooms	C4

Key to Town Plan

ΛΛ Rooommondod roads	
Other roads	
Restricted roads	
Buildings of interest	
Churches	†
Car parks	P
Parks and open spaces	
AA Service Centre	AA

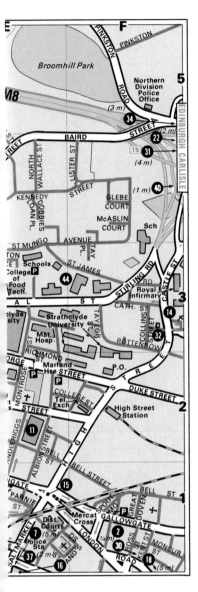

Street Index and Grid Reference

Central Glasgow

DIRECTORY

*The Griffin pub stands in Charing Cross opposite the
King's Theatre in an area well supplied with traditional
pubs and fine restaurants*

Using the Directory

*The practical information in this Directory, including addresses, telephone numbers
and opening times, is liable to change at short notice.
While every effort has been made to ensure that it is comprehensive and
up to date, the publishers cannot accept responsibility for errors or
omissions, or for changes in the details given.*

TELEPHONE NUMBERS
There is no need to dial 041 when telephoning within Glasgow.

AA CLASSIFICATIONS

Hotels

★　Good hotels and inns, generally of small scale and with good furnishings and facilities.

★★　Hotels with a higher standard of accommodation. There should be 20% private bathrooms or showers.

★★★　Well-appointed hotels. Two-thirds of the bedrooms should have private bathrooms or showers.

★★★★　Exceptionally well-appointed hotels offering high standards of comfort and service. All bedrooms should have private bathrooms or showers.

★★★★★　Luxury hotels offering the highest international standards.

Restaurants

✕　Modest but good restaurant.

✕✕　Restaurant offering a higher standard of comfort than above.

✕✕✕　Well-appointed restaurant.

✕✕✕✕　Exceptionally well-appointed restaurant.

✕✕✕✕✕　Luxury restaurant.

Rosettes
The rosette award is used to highlight hotels and restaurants where it is judged that the food and service can be especially recommended.

❀　The food is of a higher standard than is expected for its classification.

❀❀　Excellent food and service, irrespective of its classification.

❀❀❀　Outstanding food and service, irrespective of its classification.

Abbreviations

AM　Ancient Monuments in Scotland are the responsibility of the Scottish Development Department, 3–11 Melville St, Edinburgh EH3 7QD. Membership of the Friends of the Scottish Monuments can be purchased from the above address.

BH　Bank Holidays
ch 15 20p　children under 15 20p
ch 20p　children 20p
ER　Egon Ronay
Etr　Easter
ex　Except
Free　Admission free
NTS　National Trust for Scotland
Pen　Senior Citizens
PH　Public Holidays
*　1986–87 information

For more details on the accommodation and eating out establishments listed, please see the current edition of the AA guides:
*Hotels and Restaurants in Britain;
Guesthouses, Farmhouses and Inns in Britain
Holiday Homes, Cottages and Apartments in Britain,*
and the Egon Ronay guides:
*Healthy Eating Out;
Pub Guide;
Just a Bite
Egon Ronay's Guide to Hotels,
Restaurants and Inns.*

Annual events

January	Pantomime	*July*	Glasgow Folk Festival Carnival—Glasgow Green
May	Mayfest Paisley Festival Clyde Festival Scottish Cup Final	*August*	World Pipe Band Championship Bellahouston Park
June	SNO Proms Jazz Festival Glasgow Heritage Week Glasgow Show (formerly Horse Show & Country Fair)	*September*	Glasgow Marathon
		October	Modern Homes Exhibition
June	Lord Provost's Procession	*December*	Pantomime

How to get there

AIR SERVICES

Planes fly to and from Glasgow from the following airports

London:

Gatwick	British Caledonian
Heathrow	British Airways, British Midland

Other UK airports:

Birmingham	British Airways
East Midlands	British Midland
Isle of Man	Manx Airlines
Leeds	Brown Air
Manchester	Loganair, British Airways
Southampton	British Airways
Wick (Highland)	British Airways

Channel Islands:

Guernsey	British Airways
Jersey	British Airways, British Midland

Ireland:

Belfast	Air Ecosse, British Airways, Loganair
Cork	British Airways
Dublin	Aer Lingus

There are regular services between Glasgow Airport, Abbotsinch and both Anderston Bus Station and Buchanan Bus Station.

BRITISH RAIL

Frequent Intercity express trains operate daily from Euston to Glasgow; the journey takes approximately 5 hours.

BY ROAD

Glasgow is approached from the south via the M6, A74, M74 and M8 motorways; from Edinburgh via the A80 and M8 motorway; and from Fort William and the north-west via the A82.

Accommodation

HOTELS

CITY CENTRE
★★★**Albany** Bothwell St *041-248 2656* Telex no 77440
★★★**Holiday Inn Glasgow** Argyle St, Anderston *041-226 5577* Telex no 776355
★★★**Hospitality Inn** 36 Cambridge St *041-332 3311* Telex no 777334
★★★★**Stakis Grosvenor** Grosvenor Ter, Great Western Rd *041-339 8811* Telex no 776247
★★★**Bellahouston Swallow** 517 Paisley Road West *041-427 3146* Telex no 778795
★★★**Crest Hotel Glasgow-City** Argyle St *041-248 2355* Telex no 779652
★★★**Stakis Burnbrae** Milngavie Rd, Bearsden *041-942 5951*

★★★**Stakis Ingram** Ingram St *041-248 4401* Telex no 776470
★★★**Stakis Pond** Great Western Rd *041-334 8161* Telex no 776573
★★**Tinto Firs Thistle** 470 Kilmarnock Rd *041-637 2353* Telex no 778329
★★**Ewington** 132 Queens Dr, Queens Park *041-423 1152*
★★**Newlands** 260 Kilmarnock Rd *041-632 9171*
★★**Sherbrooke** 11 Sherbrooke Ave, Pollokshields *041-427 4227* Closed 1 & 2 Jan
★★**Wickets** 52–4 Fortrose St, Partickhill *041-334 9334* Closed 1 Jan

GLASGOW AIRPORT
★★★**Excelsior** Abbotsinch, Paisley *041-887 1212* Telex no 777733

★★★**Crest Hotel Erskine Bridge** North Barr, Inchinan *041-812 0123*
★★★**Dean Park** 91 Glasgow Rd, Renfrew (3m NE A8) *041-886 3771* Telex no 779032
★★★**Glynhill** Paisley Rd, Renfrew (2m E A741) *041-886 5555* Telex no 779536
★★★**Stakis Normandy** Inchinan Rd, Renfrew (2m NE A8) *041-886 4100* Telex no 778897
★★**Ardgowan** Blackhall St, Lonend, Paisley *041-887 2196*
★★**Rockfield** 125 Renfrew Rd, Paisley (2m SE off A741) *041-889 6182* Closed 25, 26 Dec & 1 Jan

GUESTHOUSES

Dalmeny Hotel 62 Andrews Dr, Nithsdale Cross *041-427 1106*

Kelvin Private Hotel 15 Buckingham Ter, Hillhead *041-339 7143*

Linwood Hotel 356 Albert Dr, Pollokshields *041-427 1642* Mar–Nov

Marie Stuart Hotel 46–8 Queen Mary Ave, Cathcart *041-424 3939* Closed 25 Dec & 1 Jan

Smith's Hotel 963 Sauchiehall St *041-339 6363*

SELF-CATERING

Mr S Taylor **White House**

12 Cleveden Crescent, Glasgow G12 0PA *041-339 9375* Flats for 1–4 people in a listed Edwardian town house with full chambermaid service

YOUTH HOSTELS

(Not AA appointed accommodation) Low-priced accommodation for members of the Youth Hostels Association. Membership can be obtained from any hostel or from the Scottish Youth Hostels Association, address below:

Scottish Youth Hostels Association 12 Renfield Street, G2 *041-226 3976*

YMCA 33 Petershill Drive, G21 *041-558 6166*

YMCA 1161 Tollcross Road, G32 *041-763 1611*

YWCA 2 Somerset Place, G3 *041-332 8365*

YWCA 36 Muslin Street, G40 *041-556 3033*

(ER indicates Egon Ronay-appointed establishments)

Eating and drinking out

RESTAURANTS—The AA's choice

CITY CENTRE

✕✕✕**Ambassador** 19–20 Blythswood Sq *041-221 2034* International cooking

✱✕✕✕**Fountain** 2 Woodside Cres *041-332 6396* Closed Sun. Lunch not served Sat. Dinner not served Mon. French cooking

✕✕**L'Arosto Ristorante** 92–4 Mitchell St *041-221 0971* Closed Sun. Italian cooking

✱✕✕**Buttery** 652 Argyle St *041-221 8188* Closed Sun. Lunch not served Sat. French cooking

✕✕**Colonial** 25 High St *041-552 1923* Closed Sun, 25, 26 Dec, 1–4 Jan & 18 Jul–3 Aug. Lunch not served Sat. Dinner not served Mon. French cooking

✕✕**Kensingtons** 164 Darnley St, Pollokshields *041-424 3662* Closed Sun & Mon. Lunch not served Sat. International cooking

✕✕**Koh-i-Noor** 235 North St *041-221 1555* Indian cooking

✕✕**Poachers** Ruthven Ln *041-339 0932*

Closed Sun

✕✕**Rogano** 11 Exchange Pl *041-248 4055* Closed Sun, 25, 26 Dec, 1 Jan and Bank Hols. French cooking

✕✕**Shish Mahal** 45 Gibson St *041-334 7899* English, Indian & Pakistani cooking

✕**Basement at Archie's** 27 Waterloo St *041-221 0551* Closed Sun. Lunch not served Sat. European cooking

✕**Loon Fung** 417 Sauchiehall St *041-332 1240* Cantonese cooking

✕**Peking Inn** 191 Hope St *041-332 8971* Closed Sun & Chinese New Year. Cantonese & Pekinese cooking

✕**Peppino's** 11–13 Hyndland St, Partick *041-339 6523* Closed Sun, Mon, last 2 wks Jul & 1st wk Aug. French & Italian cooking

✕**Trattoria Caruso** 313 Hope St *041-331 2607* Closed Sun & 1st 2 wks Aug. Italian cooking

✕**Trattoria Sorrento** 87 Kilmarnock Rd, Shawlands *041-649 3002* Closed Xmas & New Year. Lunch not served Sun. French & Italian cooking

GLASGOW AIRPORT

✕**Peking Rendezvous** 40 Old Sneddon St, Paisley *041-848 1333*

OTHER RECOMMENDED RESTAURANTS (ER)

Amber 130 Byres Rd *041-339 6121* Closed for lunch Sun & 3 days for Chinese New Year. Chinese cooking

LIGHT MEALS AND SNACKS (ER)

Cafe Gandolfi 64 Albion St *041-552 6813* Closed Sun & Bank Hols

De Quincey's/Brahms & Liszt 71 Renfield St *041-333 0633* Closed Sun & Bank Hols

Joe's Garage 52 Bank St *041-339 5407* Closed 1 & 2 Jan, 25 & 26 Dec

Tom Sawyer's 242 Woodlands Rd *041-332 5687* Closed 1 Jan & 25 Dec

Ubiquitous Chip 2 Ashton Ln, off Byres Rd *041-334 5007* Closed Sun, 1 Jan & 25 Dec

Warehouse Café 61 Glassford St *041-552 4181* Closed Sun & BH

PUB FOOD (ER)

Babbity Bowster 16 Blackfriars St *041-552 5055*

The name you can trust for Tandoori and curried dishes.
Also take away service available.
Open 11.45am till 11.30pm.

45 Gibson Street, Glasgow G12.
Tel. 041-339 8256 or 041-334 7899

Places to visit

CITY CENTRE

Annan Gallery 130 West Campbell St *041-221 5087* Open Mon–Fri 9–5, Sat 9.30–12.30

Bellahouston Park Ibrox *041-427 4224* (park) *041-427 0558* (sports centre) Open daily end Apr–Aug 8–10, Sep–Apr 8–5 (times approximate). Free

Botanic Gardens (off Great
Western Rd) *041-334 2422*
The Kibble Palace open 10–4.45
(4.15 in winter) The main
glasshouse open Mon–Sat 1–
4.45 (4.15 in winter), Sun 12–
4.45 (4.15 in winter) Gardens
open daily 7am–dusk. Free

The Burrell Collection Pollok
Country Park *041-649 7151*
Open Mon–Sat 10–5, Sun 2–5
(closed 25 Dec & 1 Jan). Free

**Charles Rennie Mackintosh
Centre** (formerly Queen's Cross
Church) 870 Garscube Rd *041-
946 6600*
Open Tues, Thu & Fri 12–5.30,
Sun 2.30–5 or by appointment

City Chambers George Square
041-221 9600
Guided tours Mon, Tue, Wed &
Fri at 10.30 and 2.30 (subject to
functions). Free

Crookston Castle (AM)
Brockburn Rd   *041-883 9606*
Open Apr–Sep Mon–Sat 9.30–7,
Sun 2–7; Oct–Mar Mon–Sat
9.30–4, Sun 2–4 (closed Thu &
Fri in winter)
*50p (ch & pen 25p)

George Square

**Glasgow Art Gallery and
Museum** Kelvingrove Park
041-357 3929
Open Mon–Sat 10–5, Sun 2–5
(Closed 25 Dec & 1 Jan). Free

Glasgow Cathedral (AM)
Castle St
Open Apr–Sep Mon–Sat 9.30–
7, Sun 2–7; Oct–Mar Mon–Sat
9.30–4, Sun 2–4. Free

**Glasgow Cross and Tolbooth
Steeple**

Glasgow Green Saltmarket

Glasgow Necropolis John Knox
St *041-552 8819*
Open daily 8am–8pm; office
(adjacent to house at west end of
Bridge of Sighs) Mon–Fri 8–
4.30, Sat 8–12 noon. Free

Glasgow Print Studio 128 Ingram
St *041-552 0704*
Open Mon–Sat 10–5.30

Glasgow School of Art
167 Renfrew St *041-332 9797*
Escorted tours when staff
available
Open Mon–Fri 10.30–11.30,
2.30–3.30 term time only

Glasgow Zoo Calderpark *041-
771 1185*
Open all year daily 10–5 (or 6
depending on season) £2 (ch,
pen, students & unemployed £1,
ch 3 free)

Glengoyne Distillery Lang
Brothers Ltd 100 West Nile St
041-332 6361
Guided tours Mon–Fri 10.30am,
11.15am, 12noon, 2pm, 3.15pm
Parties over 10 must book in
advance

Haggs Castle 100 St Andrews
Drive *041-427 2725*
Open Mon–Sat 10–5, Sun 2–5
(closed 25 Dec & 1 Jan). Free.
Guided tours only if booked in
advance

**The High Court and Jocelyn
Square** *041-552 0317* Open to
public when in session

Hunterian Art Gallery The
University of Glasgow *041-
330 5431*
Main gallery open Mon–Fri
9.30–5, Sat 9.30–1 Mackintosh
House Mon–Fri 9.30–12.30 &
1.30–5, Sat 9.30–1 (telephone
for details of public holiday
closures). 50p (the Mackintosh
House on weekday afternoons &
Sat mornings) Other areas free

Hunterian Museum The
University of Glasgow *041-
330 4221*
Open Mon–Fri 9.30–5, Sat
9.30–1 (telephone for details of
public holiday closures). Free

Hutchesons' Hall (NTS)
158 Ingram St *041-552 8391*
Visitor Centre open Mon–Fri
9–5, Sat 10–4. Shop Mon–Sat
10–4. Free

Linn Park Cathcart (southern
outskirts of Glasgow) *041-
637 1147*
Open daily 7am–dusk. Free

Merchants' House 7 West George
St
Open May–Sep Mon–Fri 10–4,
when meetings not in progress

Metro Gallery 713 Great Western
Road *041-339 0737*
Open Tue–Sat 10.30–5

The Mitchell Library North St
041-221 7030
Open Mon–Fri 9.30–9, Sat
9.30–5

**Museum for the 602 (City of
Glasgow) Squadron** Queen
Elizabeth Ave, Hillington *041-
882 6201 ext 105*
Open Wed & Fri 7.30pm–
9.30pm, 1st Sun of each month
2–5

Museum of Education Scotland
Street School *041-552 8819*
Open Mon–Sat 10–5, Sun 2–5.
Free

Museum of Transport Kelvin
Hall. Due to open
Spring 1988

People's Palace Museum
Glasgow Green *041-554 0223*
Open Mon–Sat 10–5, Sun 2–5
(closed 25 Dec & 1 Jan).
Free

Pollok Country Park *041-632 9299*
Park always open.
Demonstration and display
garden open daily Mon–Thu 8–
4, Fri 8–3. Weekends 8–6.30
(Etr–Sep), 8–4 (Oct–Etr).
Free

Pollok House *041-632 0274*
Open Mon–Sat 10–5, Sun 2–5
(closed 25 Dec & 1 Jan). Free

Provan Hall Auchinlea Rd *041-
771 6372*
Telephone for details of opening
times. Free

Provand's Lordship 3 Castle St
041-552 8819
Open all year Mon–Sat 10–5,
Sun 2–5 (closed 25 Dec & 1
Jan). Free

Queen's Park Victoria Rd

**Regimental Museum of the
Royal Highland Fusiliers**
518 Sauchiehall St
Open Mon–Thu 9–4.30, Fri 9–
4 (closed public holidays).
Free

Rosshall Park Crookston *041-
882 3554*
Open Apr–Sep daily 1–8; Oct–
Mar daily 1–4. Free

Rutherglen Museum Rutherglen
041-647 0837
Open all year daily Mon–Sat
10–5, Sun 2–5 (closed 25 Dec &
1 Jan). Free

St Andrew's RC Cathedral
172 Clyde St

St George's Tron Church
Buchanan St

Scottish Design Centre 72 St
Vincent St *041-221 6121*
Open Mon–Fri 9.30–5,
Sat 9–5

St Vincent Street Free Church
265 St Vincent St

The Stock Exchange Nelson
Mandela Place (formerly St
George's Place) *041-221 7060*
Open Mon–Fri 10–12.45 & 2–
3.30 Visitors' gallery

Tenement House (NTS) 145
Buccleuch St, Garnethill (N of
Charing Cross) *041-333 0183*
Open Jan–16 Apr, Sat & Sun
2–4; 17 Apr–Oct daily 2–5;
Nov–Mar Sat & Sun 2–4. £1
(ch 50p)

Third Eye Centre 350 Sauchiehall St *041-332 7521*
Open Tue–Sat 10–5.30, Sun 2–5.30. Free

The Trades House 85 Glassford Street
Open Mon–Fri 10–5 (closed public holidays)

The Tron Steeple Trongate

Victoria Park Whiteinch *041-959 1146*
Fossil Grove Building open Mon–Fri 8–4, Sat & Sun pm only. Park open daily 7am–dusk. Free

PS Waverley Anderston Quay *041-221 8152* for details of excursions

AROUND GLASGOW

Auchentoshan Distillery Dalmuir, Clydebank, G81 *(0389) 79476*
Distillers of triple distilled lowland single malt whisky. Visitors welcome

Balloch Castle Country Park *(0389) 58216*
Open Visitor centre Apr–Sep daily 10–6, Country Park 8am–dusk, garden 10–9 (4.30 winter). Free

Bothwell Castle (AM) Entrance at Uddington Cross by traffic lights
Open Apr–Sep weekdays 9.30–7, Sun 2–7; Oct–Mar weekdays 9.30–4, Sun 2–4 (closed Thu afternoon & Fri in winter) 50p (ch & pen 25p)

Cambuskenneth Abbey (AM) Stirling
Open Apr–Sep Mon–Sat 9.30–7, Sun 2–7 50p (ch & pen 25p)

Coats Observatory 49 Oakshaw St, Paisley *041-889 3151*
Open Mon–Fri 2–5, Sat 10–1 & 2–5; Jan–Mar Thu 7pm–9pm weather permitting. Public holidays 2–5 (closed Xmas & New Year). Free

Colzium House and Estate Kilsyth *(0236) 823281*
House open Etr weekend–Sep weekend, Mon–Fri 9–5, Sun 10–6, (closed when booked for private functions). Grounds open at all times. Museum open Wed 2–8. Free

Culcreuch Castle and Country Park, Fintry *(036086) 228*
Estate open daily 11–dusk. Castle open Sun with only guided tour at 2.15 and 3.45. Castle tours £1. Estate & gardens free

David Livingstone Centre (with the Livingstone Memorial)
Blantyre *(0698) 823140*
Open daily Mon–Sat 10–6, Sun 2–6. Last admission 5.15 *£1 (ch & pen 50p)

Dean Castle Dean Rd, Kilmarnock *(0563) 26401 ext 36*
Open 12 May–22 Sep Mon–Fri 2–5, Sat & Sun 12–5. Last entry 4.30 *£1 (ch 16 & pen free)

Dick Institute Elmbank Ave Kilmarnock *(0563) 26401*
Open

Dumbarton Castle (AM)
Open Apr–Sep weekdays 9.30–7, Sun 2–7; Oct–Mar weekdays 9.30–4, Sun 2–4 *50p (ch & pen 25p)

Eglinton Castle and Gardens Irvine Rd, Kilwinning, Irvine *(0294) 74166 ext 373*
Open all year during daylight hours. Free

Falkirk Museum *(0324) 24911 ext 2472*
Open Mon–Sat 10.30–12.30, 1.30–5. Free

Greenbank Garden (NTS) Clarkston (off B767 on southern outskirts of city) *041-639 3281*
Garden open all year daily 9.30–sunset. Garden advice Thu 2–5 (at garden or by phone) £1 (ch 16 50p)

Hamilton District Museum 129 Muir St *(0698) 283981*
Open Mon–Sat 10–5. Free

Heckling Shop Glasgow Vennel, Irvine *(0294) 75059*
Access through the premises of the Ayrshire Writers & Artists Society at No 10 Glasgow Vennel.
Open Mon–Sat 10–5

The Hill House (NTS) Upper Colquhoun St, Helensburgh *(0436) 3900*
Open daily 1–5 (closed Xmas & New Year) £1.50 (ch 90p)

Kelburn Country Centre, Largs (2m S off A78) Fairlie *(047556) 685 or 554*
Open Etr–mid Oct, daily 10–6; mid Oct–Etr Sun only 11–6 £1.50 (ch & pen £1)

Lochwinnock Community Museum Main St *(0505) 842615*
Open Mon, Wed & Fri 10–1, 2–5 & 6–8; Tue & Sat 10–1 & 2–5. Free

Mar's War (AM) Broad St, Stirling. Open at all times. Free

McLean Museum and Art Gallery 9 Union St, Greenock *(0475) 23741*
Open Mon–Sat 10–12 & 1–5. Free

The Museum of the Argyll & Sutherland Highlanders, Stirling Castle, Upper Castle Hill *(0786) 75165*
Open Etr–Sep Mon–Sat 10–5.30, Sun 11–5; Oct Mon–Fri 10–4. Free

Paisley Museum and Art Galleries High St *041-889 3151*
Open Mon–Sat 10–5 (Closed Public Holidays). Free

Roman Bath-house (AM) Roman Rd, Bearsden.
Open at all reasonable times. Free

Rough Castle, Falkirk (AM)
Accessible at any reasonable time. Free

Rouken Glen Park Thornliebank *041-638 1101*
Open daily dawn–dusk. Free

Scottish Maritime Museum Laird Forge Building, Gottries Rd, Irvine *(0294) 78283*
Open Mar–mid Oct daily 10–4 50p (ch 25p, family ticket £1)

Skelmorlie Aisle (AM) Largs
Open Apr–Sep weekdays 9.30–7, Sun 2–7. Closed winter 50p (ch & pen 25p)

Stirling Castle (AM) Upper Castle Hill
Open 4 Jan–23 Mar & Oct–Dec, Mon–Sat 9.30–4.20 last ticket sold, Sun 12.30–3.35 last ticket sold; 24 Mar–Sep Mon–Sat 9.30–5.15 last ticket sold, Sun 10.30–5.30 last ticket sold. Castle closes 45 mins after above times. £1.20 (ch & pen 60p)

Stirling Castle Vistor Centre *(0786) 62517*
Open 24 Mar–Sep, Mon–Sat 9.30–5.15, Sun 10.30–4.45; Feb–23 Mar & Oct–Dec, Mon–Sat 9.30–4.20, Sun 12.30–3.35
Charge for audio visual presentation of the history of Stirling Castle

Stirling Smith Art Gallery and Museum 40 Albert Place, Dumbarton Rd *(0786) 71917*
Open Wed–Sun 2–5 (10.30–Sat). Free

Wallace Monument Causewayhead *(0786) 72140*
Open Feb, Mar & Oct 10–5; Apr & Sep 10–6; May, Jun, Jul & Aug 10–7. £1 (ch 50p)

Weaver's Cottage (NTS) Kilbarchan *(05057) 5234*
Open Apr–May, Sep–29 Oct, Tue, Thu, Sat & Sun 2–5; Jun–Aug daily 2–5. Last admission 4.30. 80p (ch 40p)

Entertainment

112

CINEMAS

ABC Cinema 326 Sauchiehall St *041-332 9513*

Glasgow Film Theatre, 12 Rose St *041-332 6535*

Odeon Film Centre, 56 Renfield St *041-332 8701*

DISCOS AND NIGHTCLUBS

Bennetts, 90 Glassford St *041-552 5761* Tue & Thu 11pm–3am

Fri–Sun 11pm–3.30am

Cardinal Folly, 193 Pitt St *041-332 1111* Thu & Sun 10pm–2.30am, Fri & Sat 10.30pm–3am. Over 21s

Cleopatras, 508 Great Western Rd

041-334 0560 Fri & Sat 10pm–
2.30am, Sun 10pm–2am
Club de France, Russell Colt St,
Coatbridge *(0236) 28264* Fri &
Sun 10pm–2.30am, Sat
10.30pm–3am
Cotton Club, 5 Scott St *041-
332 0712* Wed–Sun 11pm–
3.30am. Over 21s
Cotton Club, Lounsdale Rd,
Paisley *041-889 2276* Thu
10.30pm–2.30am, Fri & Sat
10pm–4am, Sun 10pm–2am.
Over 21s
Fury Murrys, 96 Maxwell St *041-
221 6511* Wed, Thu, Sun
10.30pm–3am, Fri & Sat
10.30pm–3.30am. Live bands
The Garage, 22 Bridge St, Paisley
041-889 7687 Mon 7pm–10.30pm
Kids' Disco (14–17yrs), 11pm–
2.30am adults, Wed & Thu
10.30pm–2.30am, Fri–Sun
10pm–2.30am.
Over 18s
The Gardens Night Club, Bank
St *(0236) 23217* Fri & Sat
9.30pm–2.30am
Henry Afrikas, 15 York St *041-
221 6111* Wed–Sat 10.30pm–
4am. Over 21s
Hollywood Studio, 9 Brown St
041-248 6606 Open daily 10pm–
3am
Joe Paparazzi, 520 Sauchiehall St
041-331 2111 Thu–Sun 11pm–
3.30am. Over 20s
Lucifers, 22 Jamaica St *041-
248 4600* Fri & Sat 11pm–
3.30am. Over 18s
Mardi Gras, 81–5 Dunlop St *041-
248 7810* Wed–Sun 10.30pm–
late
Pharaoh's, Sunnyside Rd,
Coatbridge *(0236) 31583*
Pzazz, 23 Royal Exchange Square
041-221 5323 Fri & Sat 10.30pm–
3.30am
Raffles, 15 Benalder St *041-334 5321*
Thu Jazz/Soul night 10pm–
2am, Fri & Sat 10pm–3am.
Over 18s
Rooftops, 92 Sauchiehall St *041-
332 5883* Thu–Sun 10pm–
3.30am. Live music regularly.
Over 18s
Savoy, Savoy Centre, Sauchiehall
St *041-332 0751* Mon, Thu–Sat
10.30pm–3am; Sun 10.30pm–
2.30am. Over 21s (over 25s Mon
& Thu)
Tin Pan Alley, 39 Mitchell St *041-
221 5275* Thu–Sun 8pm–3.30am

Toledo Junction, 20 New St,
Paisley *041-887 3691* Fri–Mon
10pm–2.30am, Mon Funk night.
Over 21s
Ultratheque, 150 Wellington St
041-332 9193 Fri & Sat 10.30pm–
3am, Sun 10.30pm–2.30am.
Over 21s
Vics, 22–6 McDowall St,
Johnstone *(0505) 25145* Thu
10pm–12.45am, Fri & Sat
10pm–1.30am. Over 18s
Warehouse Speakeasy,
75 Dunlop St *041-221 3623* Tue,
Thu & Sun 10.30pm–4am, Wed
10.30pm–3.30am, Fri 10pm–
3.30am, Sat 10.30pm–3am
Zanzibar, 506 Sauchiehall St *041-
332 0992* Wed 11.30pm–3am,
Thu–Sat 9.30pm–3am

MUSIC VENUES

COUNTRY AND WESTERN
Grand Old Opry, 2–4 Govan Rd,
041-429 5396 Fri–Sun 7.30pm–
midnight
**New Alamo Country & Western
Club,** Dunbeth Rd, Coatbridge
(0236) 23554 Dates vary
Trading Post, Carlton Place *041-
429 3445* Mon & Fri 7.30pm–
11pm

FOLK AND JAZZ
Baby Grand, Elmbank Gardens
041-248 4942 Jazz Tue–Sat
evenings
Bad Ass Club, 7–17 Clyde Place
041-429 4422 Jazz Mon evenings
Blue Note, Briggait Centre, Clyde
St *041-552 6027* Jazz Tue–Sat
evenings
Bonhams Wine Bar, Byres Rd
041-357 3424 Jazz Sun lunchtimes
Cotton Club, Lounsdale Rd,
Paisley *041-889 2276* Jazz Sun
afternoons
Duke of Touraine, 134 Ingram St
041-552 0141 Jazz Mon–Sat,
piano bar
Glasgow Society of Musicians,
73 Berkeley St *041-221 6112* Jazz
Sat from 2pm
Halt Bar, 160 Woodlands Rd *041-
332 1210* Music most nights
Kelvin Park Lorne Hotel, 923
Sauchiehall St *041-334 4891* Music
most nights, jazz Sat lunchtime
Midas, 142a St Vincent St *041-
204 0169* Jazz Sat lunchtime

Paisley Folk Club, Ardgowan
Hotel, Lonend, Paisley *041-889
3195* Folk Sun evenings
Pythagoras, 410 Sauchiehall St
041-332 3495 Jazz Wed evenings
Riverside Club, Fox St (off Clyde
Street) *041-248 3244* Jazz and
folk, check dates with venue
La Ronde, Gartsherrie Rd,
Coatbridge *(0236) 21741* Folk,
check dates with venue
Shadows, 73 Bath St *041-332 0352*
Jazz Sat afternoon and
occasional evenings
Stage Door, Gorbals St *041-
429 0922* Folk Mon evenings
Star Folk Club, 44 Carlton Place
041-429 2558 Thu evenings
La Taniere, Fox St (off Clyde
Street) *041-221 4844* Sat
afternoons and other dates
Tolbooth Bar, 11 Saltmarket *041-
552 4149* Music most nights
Tron Theatre Club, Parnie St *041-
552 4267* Jazz Sun lunchtimes,
folk Wed evenings
Victoria Bar, 159 Bridgegate *041-
552 6040* Music most nights

THEATRES AND CONCERT HALLS

The Citizen's Theatre, Gorbals St
041-429 0022/8177 Repertory
theatre
The City Hall, Candleriggs *041-
552 5961* Performances from the
Scottish National Orchestra to
folk music
The Glasgow Theatre Club,
Tron Theatre, 38 Parnie St *041-
552 3748* Contemporary drama,
musical events
The Henry Wood Hall,
Claremont St *041-552 5961* Home
of the Scottish National
Orchestra
The Kings Theatre, Bath St *041-
552 5961* Drama, music events,
amateur shows
The Mitchell Theatre, Granville
St *041-552 5961* Amateur drama
productions
The Pavilion Theatre, Renfield St
041-332 1846 Family
entertainment, variety, rock and
pop concerts, pantomime
The Theatre Royal, Hope St *041-
331 1234* Home of Scottish
Opera, performances by the
Scottish Ballet, Scottish Theatre
Company, The National
Theatre, Ballet Rambert

Recreation and sports

The parks listed below are open
8am–dusk but the recreational
facilities within them may only be
available at certain times.

Alexandra Park Cumbernauld
Road, G31 Bowling, tennis,
putting, boating, golf
Barshaw Park Glasgow Road,
Paisley Bowling, tennis, putting,
golf, boating, nature corner,
model railway, BMX cycle track

Bellahouston Park Paisley Road
West, G51 Bowling, tennis
putting, golf, dry ski slope,
indoor sports centre
Brodie Park Braids Road, Paisley
Bowling, tennis, pitch and putt

Cowan Park Darnley Road, Barrhead Bowling, tennis, putting

Glasgow Green Saltmarket, G40 Bowling, tennis, putting

Hogganfield Loch Park Cumbernauld Road, G33 Bowling, pitch and putt, windsurfing

Kelvingrove Park Kelvin Way, G12 Bowling, tennis, putting, croquet

Linn Park Simshill Road, G44 Putting, nature trail, nature corner, pony trekking

Queen's Park Queen's Drive, G42 Bowling, tennis, putting, boating

Robertson Park Inchinnan Road, Renfrew Bowling, tennis, putting

Victoria Park Victoria Park Drive South, G11 Bowling, tennis, putting, boating, crazy golf, croquet, boating, arboretum, Fossil Grove

Woodhead Park Lenzie Road, Kirkintilloch Putting, table tennis, trampolines, aviary, glasshouses

CRICKET

Cartha Cricket Club Haggs Road, G41

Clydesdale Cricket Club Beaton Road, G41

Poloc Cricket Club Shawholm 2060 Pollokshaws Road, G43

West of Scotland Cricket Ground Peel Street, G11

FISHING

LOCHS AND RESERVOIRS

Banton Loch Kilsyth. Brown trout season 15 Mar–6 Oct. Permits from: Colzium Sales & Services Station, Stirling Road, Kilsyth. Boats from: Coachman Hotel, Kilsyth

Hillend Reservoir Caldercruix. Brown and rainbow trout season 15 Mar–6 Oct. Permits from: Airdrie Angling Club, Roy Burgess 21 Elswick Drive, Caldercruix, Lanarkshire (0236) 842050

Strathclyde Country Park Loch Motherwell. Carp, bream, roach, pike, perch, dace season 17 Jan–13 Mar; grayling, trout season 15 Mar–29 Sep. Permits from: Booking Office, Strathclyde Country Park, 366 Hamilton Road, Motherwell (0698) 66155

RIVERS AND CANALS

River Clyde. Brown trout season 15 Mar–30 Sep; grayling no close season. Permits available from tackle shops in Glasgow.

Forth and Clyde Canal. Pike, perch, roach, tench, carp, no close season. Permits available from: British Waterways Board, Canal House, Applecross Street, Glasgow 041-332 6936

Garrell Burn Kilsyth. Brown trout season 15 Mar–6 Oct. Permits from: Colzium Sales & Service Station, Stirling Road, Kilsyth and Coachman Hotel, Kilsyth

FOOTBALL

Celtic Football Club Celtic Park, 95 Kerrydale Street, G40

Clyde Football Club Shawfield Park, Shawfield Drive, G5

Partick Thistle Football Club Firhill Park, Firhill Road, G20

Queen's Park Football Club Hampden Park, Somerville Drive, G42

Rangers Football Club Ibrox Park, Edmiston Drive, G51

GOLF COURSES

For more details of the golf courses listed here, please see the current edition of the *AA Guide to Golf Courses in Britain*.
Visitors are welcome at all times at the municipal courses listed below:

Alexandra Park Glasgow 041-554 4887

Barshaw Barshaw Park, Paisley 041-889 2908
1 mile east of Paisley off A737

Kings Park Croftpark Avenue, Glasgow 041-637 1066
4 miles south of city centre off B766

Knightswood Park Lincoln Avenue, Glasgow 041-959 2131
4 miles north-west of city centre off A82

Lethamhill Cumbernauld Road, Glasgow 041-770 6220
3 miles north-east of city centre on A80

Linn Park Simshill Road, Glasgow 041-637 5871
4 miles south of city centre off B766

Littlehill Auchinairn Road, Bishopbriggs 041-772 1916

Ruchill Brassey Street, Glasgow 041-946 3269

Visitors are generally welcome at the golf clubs listed below. Some clubs do impose certain restrictions and where this is the case these have been noted at the end of each entry. It is advisable to telephone in advance and check when starting times are available. Clubs and trolleys are available for hire at many clubs.

Balmore By Torrance (0360) 20240 North of Balmore off A807. Visitors welcome

Caldwell Uplawmoor (050585) 329 ½ mile south-west of Uplawmoor off A736. Visitors welcome weekdays with a letter of introduction

Campsie Crow Road, Lennoxtown (0360) 310144. ½ mile north of Lennoxtown on B822. Visitors welcome, restricted until 4pm

Cawder Cadder Estate, Bishopbriggs 041-772 7101. 1mile north-east of Bishopbriggs off A803. Visitors welcome midweek

Cochrane Castle Scott Avenue, Johnstone (0505) 20146. 1 mile

south-west of Johnstone off A737. Visitors welcome weekdays

Ferenze Ferenze Ave, Barrhead 041-881 1519. North-west side of town off B774. Visitors welcome weekdays only with a letter of introduction

Gleddoch Langbank (047554) 304 1 mile south of Langbank off B789. Visitors welcome with a letter of introduction

Lenzie 19 Crosshill Road, Lenzie 041-776 1535. South side of town on B819. Visitors are required to telephone or write to the club secretary in advance

Lochwinnoch Burnfoot Road, Lochwinnoch (0505) 842710 West side of town off A760. Visitors welcome at all times

Mount Ellen Gartcosh (0236) 872277. ¾ mile north of Gartcosh off A752. Visitors are welcome with a letter of introduction

Old Ranfurly Bridge of Weir (0505) 631612. Visitors welcome weekdays with a letter of introduction

Pollok 90 Barrhead Road, Glasgow 041-632 1080. 4 miles south-west of the city centre on A762. Visitors welcome weekdays with a letter of introduction

Ranfurly Castle Golf Road, Bridge of Weir (0505) 612609. Visitors welcome weekdays only with a letter of introduction

Renfrew Blytheswood Estate, Inchinnan Road 041-886 6692 ¾ mile west of Renfrew off A8. Visitors welcome with a letter of introduction

HORSE RIDING

Kilmardinny Riding Centre Milngavie Road, Bearsden 041-942 4404

ICE RINK

Crossmyloof Ice Rink Titwood Road, G41 041-423 3093 Ice skating, curling

RUGBY GROUNDS

Balgray (Kelvinside Academicals) Great Western Road, G12

Garscadden (Glasgow University) Garscadden Road South, G15

Hughenden (Hillhead High School) Hughenden Road, G12

New Anniesland (Glasgow Academicals) Helensburgh Drive, G13

Old Anniesland (Glasgow High School FP) Crow Road, G11

Westerlands (Glasgow University) Ascot Avenue, G12

SNOOKER

Crucible Club Anderston Centre Argyle Street 041-226 4634

Reardon Snooker Centre 177 Trongate 041-552 7177

SPORTS CENTRES

Barrhead Sports Centre Main

Street, Barrhead 041-881 1049 Indoor swimming pool, badminton, squash, sauna

Bellahouston Sports Centre Bellahouston Drive, Glasgow 041-427 5454 Badminton, carpet bowls, squash etc

Bishopbriggs Sports Centre 147 Balmuildy Road, Bishopbriggs 041-772 6391 Swimming pool, indoor bowls, archery, facilities for the disabled

Crownpoint Road Sports Park Crownpoint Road, Bridgeton 041-554 8274 Athletics park, gymnasium

Paisley Leisure Complex Bank Street, Paisley 041-889 4000 Indoor facilities including pool with wave-making machine

Pollokshaws Sports Centre Ashtree Road, Pollokshaws 041-632 2200 Badminton, carpet bowls, swimming pool, turkish suite etc

SWIMMING POOLS

Castlemilk 137 Castlemilk Drive 041-634 8254

Drumchapel 199 Drumry Road East 041-944 5812

Easterhouse Bogbain Road 041-771 7978

Govanhill 99 Calder Street 041-423 0233

Ibrox Swimming Pool Clynder Street 041-445 1288

North Woodside 10 Braid Square 041-332 6235

Shettleston Elvan Street 041-778 1346

Temple 354 Netherton Road 041-954 6537

Whitehill 240 Onslow Drive 041-551 9969

Whiteinch 140 Medwyn Street 041-959 2465

Whitevale 81 Whitevale Street 041-554 0695

Shopping

Most of the larger shops and department stores (British Home Stores, C & A, Frasers, Lewis's, Marks & Spencer) are situated in Argyle Street, Buchanan Street and Sauchiehall Street. The Barrows, the city's famous street market, off London Road is open weekends. The Argyll Arcade houses many jewellery shops and there is an antique arcade in West Regent Street.

ANTIQUE SHOPS

Douglas Fraser Antiques 203 Bath Street, G2 041-248 4220 Open Mon–Fri 10–5, Sat 10–1

G & H Gardiner 105 West Regent Street, G2 041-332 1264 Open Mon–Fri 10–5

Glasgow Print Studio 128 Ingram Street, G1 041-552 0704 Open Mon–Sat 10–5.30

Cooper Hay Rare Books 203 Bath Street, G2 041-226 3074 Open Mon–Fri 10–5, Sat 10–1

Illuminati 21 Renfield Street 041-204 2361 Open Mon–Sat 10–5.30

Mercat Antiques 246 West George Street G2 041-204 0851 Open Mon–Fri 10–5.30, Sat 12–2

Metro Gallery 713 Great Western Road, G12 041-339 0737 Open Tue–Sat 10.30–5

Muirhead Moffat Antiques 182 West Regent Street, G2 041-226 4683 Open Mon–Fri 10–12.30 & 1.30–5

Victorian Village Antiques 53–63 West Regent Street, G2 041-332 0703 Open Mon–Fri 10.30–5, Sat 10.30–1

Tim Wright Antiques 147 Bath Street, G2 041-221 0364 Open Mon–Fri 9.30–4.45

BOOKSHOPS

Automobile Association 269 Argyle Street

Wm Porteous 9 Royal Exchange Place

DRY CLEANERS

Munro 42 Howard Street, G1

Munro 164a Buchanan St, G1

J Pullar & Sons 89 Mitchell Street, G1

J Pullar & Sons 492 Sauchiehall Street, G2

SCOTTISH GOODS

The Edinburgh Woollen Mill 73–5 St George's Place, G2 Scottish woollens direct from the mill

R G Lawrie 110 Buchanan Street, G1. Tartans, gifts, crystal, glass

Loch Lomond Mill 61 King Street, G1. Kilts, Highland outfitters

McMaster Fashions, In Shops, Savoy Centre, Sauchiehall Street, G2. Ladies' and children's tartans, skirts, scarves

Pitlochry Knitwear 130 Buchanan Street, G2. Tartans, tweeds, woollens

Scottish Souvenirs In Shops, Savoy Centre, Sauchiehall Street, G2. Wide selection of Scottish souvenirs

Transport

BRITISH RAIL

Central Station and Queen Street Station 24-hr passenger enquiries 041-204 2844

Queen Street Station
Departure point for trains on the scenic West Highland Line to Oban, Fort William and Mallaig with steamer connections from Oban and Mallaig to the islands. Inter City services to Edinburgh with connections to Newcastle, York and London. Other destinations include Fife, Stirling, Perth, Dundee, Aberdeen, Inverness, Wick, Thurso, Kyle of Lochalsh, Dumbarton, Balloch for Loch Lomond, Helensburgh and Milngavie. A city Rail Link Service bus connects Queen Street and Central Station.

Central Station
Departure point for Inter City

trains to destinations in England including Carlisle, Liverpool, Preston, Manchester, Leeds, Nottingham, Crewe, Birmingham and London. Also Scottish destinations in the south and west—Kilmarnock, Dumfries, Stranraer (for Ireland via Larne), Ardrossan, Largs, Gourock and Wemyss Bay with steamer connections.

BUS SERVICES

For information on bus services in Glasgow and for details of weekly or monthly bus travel tickets contact: Travel Centre, St Enoch Square 041-226 4826

Anderston Cross Bus Station 041-248 7432
Departure point for buses to: Ardrossan, Ayr, Balloch, Blantyre, Clydebank, Dumbarton, Dumfries, Eaglesham, East Kilbride,

Edinburgh, Glasgow Airport, Gourock, Hamilton, Irvine, Kilmarnock, Lanark, Largs, Motherwell, Paisley, Prestwick, Renfrew, Wemyss Bay and many other destinations.

Buchanan Bus Station 041-332 7133/9191
Departure point for buses to: Aberfoyle, Airdrie, Bearsden, Blantyre, Coatbridge, Crieff, Cumbernauld, Drymen, Dundee, Dunfermline, East Kilbride, Edinburgh, Glasgow Airport, Glencoe, Inveraray, Leven, Milngavie, Motherwell, Perth, St Andrews, Stirling and many other destinations.

CAR HIRE

When making enquiries, ask for a fully inclusive rate to include car hire, insurance, 15% VAT, any mileage charge and any other surcharges. Also check your liability in case of any damage to the vehicle as you may have to pay the first part of a claim even if you have paid insurance.

Allied Car Rental 27 Colston Road, Bishopbriggs 041-762 1414

British Car Rental Haldanes of Cathcart, 152 Clarkston Road, G44 041-637 2366

Budget Rent-a-Car 101 Waterloo Street, G2 041-226 4141

Budget Rent-a-Car Phoenix House (Airport), Inchinnan Road, Paisley 041-887 0501

Callanders Car Rental 1057 Great Western Road, G12 041-334 4646

Central Rent-a-Car 41 Elmbank Street, G2 041-248 6285

Arnold Clark 10 Vinicombe Street, G12 041-334 9501

Arnold Clark St Georges House, St Georges Road, G3 041-332 2626

Arnold Clark 43 Allison Street, G42 041-423 9559

Arnold Clark 92 Glasgow Road, Paisley 041-889 8526

Arnold Clark 64 Kirkintilloch Road, Bishopbriggs 041-772 6481

Godfrey Davis Europcar 556 Pollokshaws Road, G41 041-423 5661

Godfrey Davis Europcar Inchinnan Road, Paisley 041-887 0414

Godfrey Davis Europcar Central Station 041-221 5257

Godfrey Davis Europcar Queen Street Station 041-332 7635

Fullers Car Hire 28 Bogmoor Place, G51 041-445 5511

Jim Neary Car Hire 15 Fairley Street, G51 041-427 5475

Alex M Ritchie 43 Nithsdale Road, G41 041-423 2961

SMT Car Rental 127 Finnieston Street, G3 041-204 2828

Swan National Car Rental 222 Broomielaw, G2 041-204 1051

Swan National Car Rental St Andrew's Drive, Glasgow Airport, Paisley 041-887 7915

Swan National Car Rental Phoenix House, Inchinnan Road, Paisley 041-889 5114

Town and Country Car Rental Dean Park Hotel, 91 Glasgow Road, Renfrew 041-885 2121

Universal Garage 367 Alexandra Parade, G31 041-554 5174

CAR PARKS

National Car Parks Ltd
Multi-storey car parks open 24 hours

Anderston Centre, capacity: 100 cars

George Street, G1 (entrance on Montrose Street), capacity: 284 cars

Waterloo Street, G2, capacity: 670 cars

Mitchell Street, G1, capacity: 248 cars

Strathclyde Regional Council
Multi-storey car parks open 24 hours unless otherwise stated

Cambridge Street, capacity: 900 cars

Anderston Cross Centre capacity: 350 cars

Charing Cross Car Park, capacity: 460 cars, open 7.30–10.30

Buchanan Car Park, capacity: 780 cars

Sauchiehall Street Centre, capacity: 420 cars, open 8–10 overnight parking 6pm–9am

Surface car parks open 24 hours

King Street/Dunlop Street Car Parks (2), capacity: 885 cars.

There are 'park and ride' facilities at the following underground stations:

Kelvinbridge
Bridge Street
Shields Road

COACH SERVICES

National Express operate a network of express coach services throughout England and Wales and into Scotland from local coach and bus stations. Details are available from any National Express office or agent. Cotter Coachline and Scottish Citylink operate motorway express services from Victoria Coach Station in London. The journey time is approximately 8 hours

Cotter Coachline 298 Regent Street, London W1 (no personal callers) 01-930 5781

Scottish Citylink 298 Regent Street, London WIR 6LE 01-636 9373

FERRIES

Caledonian MacBrayne The Ferry Terminal, Gourock PA19 (0475) 33755 Ferry services for west coast of Scotland

Western Ferries 16 Woodside Crescent, G3 041-332 9766 Islay/Jura Ferry Link

CHAUFFEUR-DRIVEN GUIDED TOURS

The companies listed here offer chauffeur-driven services, conducted by experienced guides, for individuals and small groups.

Cowan's Chauffeur Service 30 Woodlands Drive, G4 041-334 9628

Glasgow Chauffeur Drive 15 Woodrow Road, G41 041-427 6622

Little's Chauffeur Drive 1282 Paisley Road West, G52 041-883 2111

Pumpkin Sheila May, St Vincent Court, 444 St Vincent Street, G3 041-226 4872

See Scotland 17 Dalziel Drive, G41 041-427 0777

Silver Car Hire Fotheringay Service Station, Darnley Road, G41 041-424 1998

Treasures of Scotland Tours 3 Silk Street, Paisley 041-887 1143

H Winchcole 214–218 Howard Street, G1 041-552 0251

TAXI TOURS

Strathkelvin TOA 20 Crowhill Road, Bishopbriggs, G64 041-762 1011

Taxi Cab Association (Radio Taxis) Ltd 451 Lawmoor Street, G5 041-429 2900

Taxi Owners Association 6a Lynedoch Street, G3 041-332 7070

GUIDED TOUR BY COACH

Guided tours of the City of Glasgow and Loch Lomond, for tickets contact:- The Greater Glasgow Tourist Board 35/39 St Vincent Place 041-942 6453 Scottish Citylink offers a range of day and afternoon tours from Buchanan Bus Station, from May to September. Details are available from Buchanan Bus Station.

TAXIS

Glasgow Radio Taxis Association Rockvilla, Applecross Street, G4 041-557 3030

Strathkelvin Taxi Owners Association 20 Crowhill Road, Bishopbriggs, G64 041-762 1011

Taxi Cabs Association (Radio Taxis) Ltd 451 Lawmoor Street, G5 041-429 2900

Taxi Owners Association 6a Lynedoch Street, G3 041-332 0054

UNDERGROUND

The underground, a circular service, connecting the city centre with the West End and the south bank of the River Clyde, operates from Monday to Saturday (there is no Sunday service). There are 'park and ride' facilities for the motorist at the following stations:
Kelvinbridge
Bridge Street
Shields Road
Further information is available from: Strathclyde Passenger Transport Executive, Travel Centre, St Enoch Square 041-226 4826

Useful information

AUTOMOBILE ASSOCIATION

AA Centre 269 Argyle Street, Glasgow G2 8DW
Insurance Services *041-204 0711*
Travel Agency *041-204 0911*
For information *041-812 0101*

BANKS

Allied Irish Banks 51 Jamaica Street, G1 *041-204 1016*
The Bank of Nova Scotia 52 West Nile Street, G1 *041-221 9171*
Bank of Scotland 2 Vincent Place, G1 *041-221 0713*
Barclays Bank 90 St Vincent Street, G2 *041-221 9585*
Clydesdale Bank Head Office 30 St Vincent Place, G1 *041-248 7070*
Co-operative Bank 147 Buchanan Street, G1 *041-221 6934*
Lloyds Bank Argyle Street, G2 *041-221 1029*
National Westminster Bank 14 Blythswood Square, G2 *041-221 6981*
The Royal Bank of Scotland 78 Union Street, G1 *041-204 0171*
Trustee Savings Bank Scotland 39 Bothwell Street, G2 *041-221 8490*

BUREAUX DE CHANGE

Foreign exchange facilities are available at most banks, and also at:

American Express 115 Hope Street, G2 *041-226 3077*
Thomas Cook 15 Gordon Street, G1 *041-221 9431*
Bureau de Change Central Station, Gordon Street, G1 *041-226 4736*

EMERGENCIES

In life-threatening emergencies, telephone 999 from any call-box and say which service is required—Fire Brigade, Police or Ambulance. There is no charge for the call. See also *Health—Hospitals* below.

GUIDES

Scottish Tourist Guides Association
Fully trained, multi-lingual guides, reservations and enquiries:
Mrs S Buchanan, 2 Ashton Green, East Kilbride, G74 *(03552) 38094*

HEALTH

EMERGENCY DENTAL SERVICE
Glasgow Dental Hospital
378 Sauchiehall Street, G2 *041-332 7020* Not 24-hour

HOSPITALS

24-hour accident and emergency
Glasgow Royal Infirmary 82–84 Castle Street *041-552 3535*
Royal Alexandra Infirmary Barbour Park, Neilston Road, Paisley *041-887 9111*
Royal Hospital for Sick Children Yorkhill, G3 *041-339 8888*
Southern General Hospital 1345 Govan Road, G51 *041-445 2466*
Stobhill General Hospital 133 Balornock Road, G21 *041-558 0111*
Victoria Infirmary Grange Road Langside, G76 *041-649 4545*
Western Infirmary Dumbarton Road, G11 *041-339 8822*

LIBRARIES

The Mitchell Library North Street *041-221 7030*
Open Mon–Fri 9.30am–9pm, Sat 9.30am–5pm. Headquarters of Glasgow's 43 public libraries, also the largest public reference library in Europe
Stirlings Library Queen Street *041-221 1867*
Open Mon, Tue, Thu & Fri 9.30am–8pm, Sat 9.30am–1pm & 2pm–5pm Closed Wed Central lending library for the city
Commercial Library The Mitchell Library, Kent Road *041-221 7030* Reference library Open Mon–Fri 9.30am–9pm, Sat 9.30am–5pm

NEWSAGENTS

Wm Porteous 9 Royal Exchange Place, G1 Specialist newsagents

NEWSPAPERS

Morning daily
Daily Record
Glasgow Herald
Scottish Daily Express
The Scotsman
Evening daily
Evening Times
Weekly
Scottish Sunday Express
Sunday Mail
Sunday Post

PHOTOGRAPHY

Dixons 115 Union Street, G1 *041-248 5711* 24-hr developing
Dixons 38 Sauchiehall Street, G2 *041-332 7611* 24-hr developing
Foto Machine 63 Renfield Street, G2 *041-331 1090* 24-hr developing

POST OFFICES

Glasgow Head PO 1–5 George Square, G2 *041-248 2882*
Bridgeton PO 30 Main Street, G40 *041-554 3506*
Castlemilk PO 27 Dougrie Drive, G45 *041-634 7262*
Cathcart PO 3 Rhannan Road, G44 *041-637 2188*
Govan PO 18 Pearce Street, G51 *041-445 1302*
Kelvinbridge PO 532 Great Western Road, G12 *041-339 5437*
Paisley PO County Square *041-887 9341*
Pollok PO 6 Haughburn Road, G53 *041-881 1723*
Rutherglen PO 157 Main Street, G73 *041-647 6346*
Shawlands PO 1179 Pollokshaws Road, G41 *041-632 4888*
Springburn PO Springburn Shopping Centre, G21 *041-558 6475*

TV AND RADIO

BBC Television
Scottish Television
Channel Four
BBC Radio Services Radio Scotland 370m 810KHz 92.5–94.6MHz
IBA Radio Services Radio Clyde 261m 1152KHz 102.5MHz

TOILETS

The following toilets are situated in the city centre:
Bain Street
Cathedral Square (facilities for the disabled)
Clyde Street
St Vincent Place
Trongate

TOURISM INFORMATION CENTRES

The National Trust for Scotland Hutchesons' Hall, Ingram Street G1 1EJ *041-552 8391*
Scottish Development Department—Edinburgh Historic Buildings and Monuments, 3–11 Melville Street, Edinburgh EH3 7PE *031-226 2570*
Scottish Tourist Board— Edinburgh, 23 Ravelston Terrace, Edinburgh EH4 3EU *031-332 2433* No personal callers
Tourist Information Centre 35/39 St Vincent Place, Glasgow G1 2ER *041-227 4887*
Tourist Information Centre Town Hall, Abbey Close, Paisley PA1 1JS *041-889 0711*

Page numbers in **bold** indicate main entries

Acknowledgements

The publishers would like to thank the Scottish Tourist Board, the City of Glasgow District Council and the Greater Glasgow Tourist Board for their help in the preparation of this book.

All the photographs except those listed below were especially commissioned by The Automobile Association for this publication and taken by Stephen Gibson Photography.

The AA also wishes to thank the following libraries, organisations and photographers for their assistance:

Aberdeen University Library 12 Embarking at the Broomilaw; *M Adelman* 97 David Marshall Lodge; *Glasgow Museums and Art Gallery* 11 Trongate, 22 Brass bobbin stand, 23 Gothic Milanese field armour, 24 Blue porcelain vase, 34 Billy Connolly; *D Hardley* 95 Rooftop devils, 94/5 Helensburgh, 95 Ben Lomond; *Hunterian Art Gallery* 23 Palaeoniscord fish; *S King* 95 Church, 97 Loch Achray; *Mary Evans Picture Library* 8/9 View of Glasgow, 33 James Brodie; *The People's Palace* 28 Poster Queen's Theatre, Poster Pavilion Theatre, 30 Seal of the Chapter of Glasgow, 31 Tobacco Lords, 32 James Maxton, 48 Votes for women; *Rex Features* 34 Kenny Dalglish; *The Scottish Ballet* 26 Romeo & Juliet; *Scottish Portrait Galleries* 10 Mary, Queen of Scots, 31 James Watt; *Eric Thorburn* 28 Orlando